AWAKEN
Sleeping Beauty

Judy Pogue

ISBN: 978-0-9996778-0-3 (Hard Back)
ISBN: 978-0-9996778-1-0 (Paper Back)

Library of Congress Control Number: 2017918136

PRINTED IN THE UNITED STATES OF AMERICA

Book Design & Layout: Russell Lake - SeedStudios.com
Cover Illustration: Malika Roberts - MalikasArtAndMurals.com
Back Cover Photos: Impressions Photography- Shannon Ireland
            On location at Drumoland Castle
Interior Illustrations: Ailbhe Cronin-Ireland - AppleBerryPress.com

First Edition December 2017

Published by:
Pogue Family Mission Society
1512 Bray Central Drive
Suite 300
McKinney, Texas 75069

AWAKEN
Sleeping Beauty

Judy has a powerful and unique ability to wake up and rekindle hope and courage in the lives of everyone she encounters. I've witnessed thousands of women (and men) have their eyes opened and hope restored as she shares out of her own trials and experiences the recurring theme of her prophetic, non-apologetic message; "the applied principals contained in God's Word can only result in His promises fulfilled". Too many women have lost sight of the beauty and the power of being a real woman. This book will help them regain some of that lost respect for femininity.

Donna Blackard
CEO, Bella Donna Chapel

Judy Pogue is one of the most interesting people I know. From building a thriving and successful construction business with her husband to being a world famous author and speaker. It's incredible now to see her traveling the world to share her story and the Gospel, and now write this powerful book that is sure to embolden women of all ages and backgrounds to be what God has made them to be.

Jeff Blackard
CEO and President, Blackard Global, Inc.

Judy Pogue's life has been all about awakening the spirit of God in everyone she meets. She exudes wisdom and caring and has the amazing gift of being able to bring the Word of God to life when she writes and speaks. Her stories are riveting; they always translate directly to everyday life. Studying under Judy has blessed me personally; I know all who read Awaken Sleeping Beauty *will be equally blessed!*

Erin Botsford
Founder and CEO, Botsford Financial Group
Author, *The Big Retirement Risk: Running of Money Before You Run Out of Time*

Judy Pogue is a beautiful woman of God who has seen the vision God has for women, to stand tall as daughters of a loving Father who has an extraordinary plan for each of our lives. Read her work, expecting a personal vision for God's perfect laid plan for your life and take hold of the miracles that are yours for the asking!

Sharla Bush
Owner, Sharla's Boutique

I'm excited to recommend Awaken Sleeping Beauty *by my friend, Judy Pogue. I've known this sweet sister for many years. In fact, because of their mission's ministry, my husband and I are ministering around the world today! Her love and passion for the Lord and His people knows no boundaries. Judy is comfortable on the big stage or in a small hut on the mission field. She loves empowering women from all walks of life and finds great joy in seeing women rise up to the full dimension of their calling. Believe me, I know firsthand! As with anything Judy does--Awaken Sleeping Beauty is current and cutting edge and will speak for generations to come!*

Becky Cruse
Worshipworks Ministries International

Every girl dreams of being a princess, right? In Awaken Sleeping Beauty, *Judy Pogue challenges us to embrace our God-given gifts, talents and abilities to live out our purpose doing 'Kingdom' work. Embrace the opportunities before you and let's get busy serving our Heavenly father, the King of all Kings.*

Jackie Green
Co-founder, Hobby Lobby
Co-founder, Museum of the Bible

I have been blessed to be a part of Judy's journey in her passion and development of the message of this book . . . from the first teachings to the art concepts . . . and even to interpret for her on several occasions in Latin America as she awoke and inspired many ladies to walk out their gifting and callings. I'm sure that you too will be awakened and challenged.

Donna Holland
International Missions Network
Ministerios Mundo de Fe

In her exciting new book Awaken Sleeping Beauty, *my friend Judy Pogue calls women to step in to the fullness and purpose that God has for every one of our lives. Judy has ministered with great power in with Latin Equip, and I am thrilled to see her message so beautifully communicated in print. Thousands have been touched by her message in Peru, and now many more thousands of women will receive God's plan to wake us from our slumber and understand our purpose as women of influence!*

Shelly Hopkins
Co-Director, Latin Equip

You'll want to read this book! An awakening is coming and Judy calls you to come alive! I've seen first hand how she gives extravagantly to touch the nations. Get ready to soar!

Klaus Kuehn
Director, Pure Worship Ministries

Women have been numbed into a place that is far less than God intended. In her book, Awaken Sleeping Beauty, *Judy Pogue is doing the work of a Prince. She is awakening sleeping women with a kiss that calls them into all that God has purposed for them. This book is perfectly timed for this generation of women. We join with her in calling women everywhere to assume their roles of partnership and leadership in this generation.*

Tom and Jan Lane
Lead Executive Senior Pastor, Apostolic Ministries - Gateway Church
Authors of *Strong Women and the Men Who Love Them*

It's easy to believe in fairytales and hope the prince sees you. In her new book, Awaken Sleeping Beauty, *Judy beautifully illustrates the truth that you're more than seen by a prince, you're loved by the true Prince of Peace.*

Debbie Morris
Executive Pastor, Gateway Church
Author - *The Blessed Woman* and
Coauthor - *The Blessed Marriage* and *Living Rightside Up*

Judy Pogue has tremendous faith and unwavering determination. She is much like Queen Esther or may I say, "Queen Esther was much like Judy Pogue."

She is a great minister and motivational speaker and also an incredible missionary to the people of Mexico and other parts of the world. I highly recommend her book and her story.

Larry Myers
Founder and President, Mexico Ministries

Judy Pogue is an advocate, coach, and champion for women, and is passionate about helping them tap into God's greatness within. Awaken Sleeping Beauty *inspires, as Judy weaves her personal story throughout the pages to reinforce that God has a special purpose for each of us and has given us the power to activate His purpose with confidence despite our circumstances. Be ready to hear God's plan to empower you for the journey.*

Linda S. Paulk
President and CEO, Sky Ranches, Inc.

If there ever was a lady destined to deliver a message of awakening to women, it is Judy Pogue. Judy exemplifies the awakened heart: watching, listening, serving and encouraging ladies to see and follow their destiny in Christ. She knows glory and she knows adversity, but most of all she knows the God who works all things together for the good of those who love Him and are called according to His purpose. Judy shows us all what it looks like to live the awakened life!

Angela Paxton
Candidate for Texas Senate 2018
Wife of Texas Attorney General Ken Paxton

Judy Pogue is being used by God to awaken the spirit of women all over the world. In Awaken Sleeping Beauty, *Judy shares personal and biblical insight on how we can all live a life full of joy, hope, restoration and abundance. God is calling all women to rise up, stand firm and embrace the gifts He's given us. He's fully equipped us to be powerful beyond measure. It's time for you to awaken, sleeping beauty and become all that He's created you to be!*

Michelle Prince
Best-Selling Author, Motivational Speaker and Publisher

From the very first time we heard Judy, we could see in her the passion and bravery she has to share this teaching to the body of Christ, showing every women the royal identity they have in Jesus. We are sure this book will challenge you to awaken from the spiritual sleep the world has wrapped you in, stand up, and help other women with your example.

Ernesto & Sandra Ramírez
Senior Pastors - Mundo de Fe México

Judy Pogue is not afraid to speak her mind. In a world full of darkness she calls all women of faith to wake up and fulfill their God given purpose. Awake Sleeping Beauty *will encourage you and challenge you to live a life of purpose. Don't just watch life pass you by...Open your eyes to see God working around you... Be open to His calling...Be adventurous and Brave...Be a vessel He can use!*

Keresa Richardson
President, Benjamin Franklin Plumbing

Judy Pogue is an amazing woman of God who is working to change our nation through prayer and instilling Biblical principles. She uses God's gifts to bring hope and encouragement to the world around her. In Awaken Sleeping Beauty, *God uses Judy's voice to wake up women, the sleeping beauties of today, from the slumber of the world to fulfill the amazing call God has for them.*

Rick Santorum
Former United States Senator

Awaken Sleeping Beauty *is a fascinating wake up call for women to pursue God's plan for their lives! You may not know what God has called you to do or perhaps you've ignored His calling for so long that you don't hear Him anymore. In this captivating book, Judy will gently urge you to stop looking at the years you've lost and look at the years you have left. You'll be driven to get intentional in your choices and start making destiny decisions to live your dreams.*

Terri Savelle Foy
President, Terri Savelle Foy Ministries
Host - *Live Your Dreams*, Author - *Pep Talk*

I have seen firsthand the life changing impact Judy Pogue has had on people around the world. Awaken Sleeping Beauty *is a timely and relevant message that will unlock the God given purpose and potential of many.*

Jonathan Shibley
President, Global Advance

In her new book, Awaken Sleeping Beauty, *Judy so eloquently paints a picture of just how much God loves you, and how valuable you are to Him. Don't miss out on these truths that will change your perspective and strengthen your identity in Jesus!*

David Shivers
Minister to Men and Evangelism, Prestonwood Baptist Church

I am honored to talk about one of the most powerful ambassadors Jesus has today. Judy Pogue made a tremendous impact in my country, Brazil, preaching in our conferences and bringing life to hundreds of woman who were sleeping and now are in the front line of Jesus's army. She also visited many businesses giving hopeless owners, ideas and faith to continue. Judy has the ability to show how simple the Gospel is and how powerful a woman is when she decides to wake up! I am sure this book is going to inspire and transform thousands around the world forever!

Paula Togni
Brazil

Judy Pogue has been used by God to help set people free around the world. She uses honest candor to break the cycle of spiritual and emotional disillusionment that have kept women asleep to their potential. This book will help wake up the Sleeping Beauty in you.

Lynton Turkington
Senior Pastor, Celebration Church

Judy Pogue is my friend and sister in Christ. I love her passion and encouragement for God's people. Every child of God is beautiful in the eyes of our Creator with a call on their lives. Satan comes to steal that call, kill our hope and destroy our life. Judy is masterful at challenging us to wake up and answer our "Call", realizing who we are, who our Father is and what He has created us to do. God has sent Judy to the nations as a dynamic conference speaker and minister of the Gospel. She has been a premier speaker in our churches for over 10 years. I honestly have never met another person so full of encouragement, passion and purpose. I strongly recommend her new book, Awaken Sleeping Beauty *to anyone looking for hope and purpose in their life. You will not be disappointed.*

Pastor David Vestal
Daybreak Ministries
President and CEO, Next Level Solution

Markree Castle
Collooney, Sligo, Ireland

ACKNOWLEDGEMENTS

I want to thank my husband Paul for his encouragement and support in writing this book. He has given me freedom to speak, to write, and to be who God has called me to be. I want to thank our sons, Randy, Brandon, and Ben, who have challenged me and loved me as only sons can. My daughters-in-law, Emily, Jennifer, and Ashleigh, have been the daughters that every mother dreams about. My heart is full with our nine grandchildren—Meredith Faith, Samantha Grace, Lincoln Paul, Alexis LeAnne, Reagan Elizabeth, Paul Maverick, Jackson Paul, Presley Grace, and Hayden Paul. You are the reason that my life is full of love and laughter.

Jonathan Shibley, Global Advance, Margi Folly and Kevin Pate—you believed in me and encouraged me to do my first international conference—thank you! I will never forget you and your encouragement.

Dana Vestal, Lena Smith, Amanda Baker, Glenda Brown, Donna Blackard, Joanna Santana, and Whitney Daugherty—you have been with me every step of the way and I will be forever thankful.

Carleen and Jim Higgins, Matt and Kari Payne—thank you for all the media and technical help. I would not have made it without you.

Most of all—to my Lord and Savior for making me his daughter and giving me the story of "Sleeping Beauty."

Bellingham Castle

Castlebellingham, Co. Louth, Ireland

TABLE OF CONTENTS

Cloghan Castle

Ballingarry, Loughrea, Co. Galway, Ireland

FOREWORD

here are people you meet in life that instantly touch your soul, who make a lasting impression on your heart and forever change the way you see life. That person for me is Judy Pogue.

I met Judy in 2013. I was introduced to her through a mutual friend to discuss an upcoming book project that my publishing company was producing. We were looking for stories of people who were "making a difference" in our community. After just a few minutes with Judy, I instantly knew she had an amazing story for this book, but I also sensed a bigger connection, a divine connection, that would later play out over the next several years.

Anyone that has ever met Judy knows she has a gift. She has the gift of knowing her identity in Christ and has a passion and natural ability to share her love of God with others. Shortly after meeting Judy, I was invited to attend her Tuesday night women's bible study in her barn. The thought of worshiping God in a barn intrigued me so I decided to check it out. To be honest, I imagined a small, dirty barn, kind of like the manger where Jesus was born. Not only was I shocked to find the "barn" was more like an event venue, but I was even more blown away by the words she spoke that forever changed my life. Week after week, I kept coming back to hear Judy's prophetic words of hope, inspiration and of God's unending love for his children. She was a breath of fresh air in my life and she probably doesn't even realize the full impact she made on me and the countless women that attended each week. I, for one, am eternally grateful that she listened to God's calling on her life.

As the years went by, we formed a beautiful friendship based on respect, admiration, and most importantly, on the mutual love of God and our passion to help women awaken to all God created them to be. Whenever I'd spend time with Judy, I'd feel a prompting in my spirit to tell her to write a book. I knew she had a story and while I didn't know the full extent of what God would do with her story, I just knew...I actually felt it, that she had a story that would impact the world. It's funny, because I didn't remember doing this until Judy reminded me of it recently, but now that I've read this amazing book, one that will totally change your life, it is confirmation that God beautifully orchestrates every detail of our lives for us to become all He has created us to be. He created us to be free, to be royalty...after all, we are daughters of The King of Kings!

I'm beyond honored and blessed to write the foreword for a book that I know will create revival in the hearts of women all over this world. Judy so eloquently shares stories of women, just like you, who have awakened from lives of frustration, busyness, and distraction. She shares biblical truths that will set us all free from the burdens of daily life and awaken us to the favor, blessings, and love that God has for each of his precious children.

I encourage you, as you read this book, to make this a defining time in your life. Decide, once and for all, to wake up and claim all that God has in store for you. It's your time. It's time to "Awaken Sleeping Beauty!"

Michelle Prince

Best-Selling Author, Zig Ziglar Motivational Speaker & Publisher

www.MichellePrince.com

Adare Manor
Adare, Co. Limerick, Ireland

1

Wake Up, Sleeping Beauty

ONCE UPON A TIME IN A LAND FAR, FAR AWAY, THERE LIVED A PRINCESS IN A ROYAL CASTLE. HER NAME WAS SLEEPING BEAUTY...

STEP BACK IN TIME WITH ME AND SEE HOW THIS MEDIEVAL STORY TOLD IN A MODERN-DAY TEXT PERTAINS TO THE WOMEN OF TODAY...

The Lord wants you—yes, *you*—to awaken from your slumber, sister.

He wants you to wipe the sleep from your eyes and the fog from your mind and become *fully awake* to the life He has created and designed for you.

He wants the women of this world who know Him as Christ to come together to move mountains. And save lives. And to live intentionally as an example for others to follow.

He wants you to fully embrace what you are to Him—a queen to be honored, a daughter to be cherished, and a woman called to live a Christ-filled life. When you accepted the call upon your life to follow Christ, you became an ambassador for His Kingdom, fully equipped and blessed beyond measure. You received the power to impact neighbors and cities and *countries* because of your calling. You are called, dear friend.

You have everything you need for your grand and extraordinary adventure. Just one thing is asked of you to accomplish this divine calling: *awaken sleeping beauty.*

I'm not one of those women who sees the hand of God in crazy, quirky things like a cross-shaped sweet potato. I don't even fully understand the whole trinity arrangement—how one person—*one being*—can be The Father, The Son, *and* The Holy Spirit *at the same time*. And I certainly don't claim to be any more supernaturally in tune with God than the next lady. Still, I've heard the voice of God speak to my spirit in loud and undeniable ways.

If you've ever experienced The Lord speaking so directly to your soul, you understand. If not, you may be thinking I had too much pizza and not enough sleep that day. I get it. I can even imagine what you're thinking right about now: "She *seems* pretty normal, but this whole hearing directly from God 'thing' is a little hard to believe. I mean, I know God works in mysterious ways and all, but *talking...to her...?*"

I get the skepticism *really,* but I also *know what I know* and that is this: *I undoubtedly heard the voice of God loud and clear.* Not audibly, mind you, but so very much deeper—*in my spirit.* The voice was so loud, so unmistakable, I could barely keep my car on the road. My heart was racing; my mind was processing a thousand thoughts a second; *and* I was going 70 mph on the interstate.

It started out as just a regular Tuesday morning and then...the Spirit of God spoke to me.

I was on my way to a luncheon honoring women involved in international missions. I was also on my way to receiving a divine appointment that would forever change the course of my life. Later that day, I even became part of the Global Advance ministries team.

More on the ministry team later; let's get back to *the voice.*

In my spirit, I heard the voice of God say to me, "Judy, I am going to use you to help wake up the sleeping beauties of the world." And that was it.

I didn't know how.

Or when.

Or to what extent.

All I knew were the words spoken to my spirit *from His Spirit.*

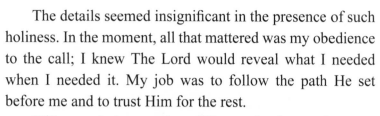

The details seemed insignificant in the presence of such holiness. In the moment, all that mattered was my obedience to the call; I knew The Lord would reveal what I needed when I needed it. My job was to follow the path He set before me and to trust Him for the rest.

Still, my mind was curious. *Who are the sleeping beauties of the world? And are they really asleep or just figuratively? And what do I know about women and their cultures half a world away?* The rational side of me wanted to know the ins and outs of what I was agreeing to; the faithful side of me was all in—follow first, ask questions later. Both sides were doing battle as I drove towards the luncheon.

If you're like me, you probably associate Sleeping Beauty as one of the Disney princesses—a pretty girl who meets with conflict, suffers a setback, and then is blissfully rescued by her very own Prince Charming. It's a theme that's worked for generations. Sure, the hair color, the skin color, and even the dress color changes from princess to princess, but that's the usual plot line for these damsels in distress. Think Cinderella, Snow White, Belle…you get the idea.

But this time was different.

In my mind, all I could picture were Hollywood celebrities and pageant winners—women known for embodying beauty and physical perfection. But this time, they weren't the picture of perfection. This time they were covered in mud and filth. It was as if they had been tossed into a pigpen—evening gowns, tiaras, and all—and what's more—they were *enjoying* wallowing in the muck and mire. They were comfortable in their surroundings. They were *where they belonged.*

Immediately the words of Proverbs 11:22 came to mind:

"Like a gold ring in a pig's snout is a beautiful woman who shows no discretion."

And also, this challenge from Proverbs 31:30:

"Charm is deceptive, and beauty is fleeting; but a woman who fears the Lord is to be praised."

The rest of the day I pondered the words I'd heard. I knew I had been chosen by God to carry this mission forward. I still didn't know how this would all play out—what my role would be, where this journey would take me, and who I would serve. All I knew at day's end was that I had received a precious gift much like the ones Moses referred to in Deuteronomy 29:29.

"The secret things belong to the Lord our God, but the things revealed belong to us and to our children forever, that we may follow all the words of this law."

I spent that evening and well into the middle of the night researching story upon story about the origin, the symbolism, and the truth behind the Sleeping Beauty fairy tale. There was so much more to the original version than what I had come to know from the Disney animated version. In the early hours of the morning, my research proved to be fruitful: I had found the hidden treasure in the story of Sleeping Beauty.

It was in the original version, written sometime in the 1400s in France, that opened my eyes—literally and spiritually—to where I felt the Lord was leading me to focus. In this version, the story tells how a young woman had been put under a curse causing her to sleep for 100 years; thus, the name Sleeping Beauty. But here's what I learned from the original story: when Sleeping Beauty fell asleep, so did her mother, her father, the nanny, the butler, the housekeepers, the gardeners, the cooks—EVERYONE in the castle! In fact, THE ENTIRE KINGDOM FELL ASLEEP!

Because she was asleep, everyone else was asleep also.

It struck a chord in my heart. When the women of this world—the mothers, the wives, the caregivers, the homemakers—fall asleep, so also do their families. And that is what was happening from continent to continent, country to country—the women of our time are content to get through their days almost as if they were in a sleep-like state. They are choosing the tranquility of comfort and acceptance over the challenge to live the lives ordained by God.

The story goes on to describe the castle and everything around it as dark, deserted, and lifeless during Sleeping Beauty's 100-year nap. What had once been a castle brimming with life and activity had become a den of darkness, covered in overgrown vines and trees and shrubs. In fact, the castle had become so overtaken by the out-of-control and unkempt brush, it was almost unrecognizable from the roadside.

> The beauty of the princess, the vitality of her family, and the majesty of her home had become so ensnared by outside forces, <u>they almost ceased to exist</u>.

In my spirit, I *knew* this is what was happening to women *everywhere*—women had fallen asleep to their calling from Christ. So many of us, myself included!, had allowed the demands of daily life, the expectations of others, and the busyness of activities to capture our vision *and* heart. It wasn't intentional or ill-meaning; *it just happened* one moment at a time, one extra commitment at a time, one moment spent worrying instead of praying. Women have let the cares of this world cause them to be silent. Their homes and their communities (which represent their personal kingdoms) have grown cold and dark without their voice.

I spent many of my years as a young mother on this trying-to-please merry-go-round. I was juggling three sons around to basketball practice, football practice, baseball games, orthodontist appointments, and all the other events surrounding their adolescent years. Plus, I was involved in PTA meetings, the church choir, and on numerous church committees. My husband and I had a growing commercial construction business that I was a vital part of, also. Somebody was always coming and going, needing help on their homework, or just shouting, "Hey, Mom, WATCH!" Some days, the best I could do was hold on tight, order pizza for dinner, and fall into bed at night *exhausted.*

I was getting by, doing the best I could; but I wasn't *thriving.*

I wasn't turning first to The Lord when things got hectic; I was handling things as best I could.

I wasn't seeing His hand in every event throughout the day; all I could focus on was the most immediate need in front of me.

And I wasn't using my God-given skills and talents to glorify Him; I was more concerned with fixing dinner than praising His name.

In short, most days my eyes were closed to Christ's presence and I had become a *sleeping beauty* racing through my own life.

But, then…then the fairy tale of *Sleeping Beauty* became real to me.

Remember the princess sleeping for the better part of a century? As long as she remained asleep, so did her family. They were technically alive, but certainly not *living.*

Until, a prince—*her* prince—let it be known that he was

going to take on the barriers that stood between him and the castle. His fellow villagers called him crazy for taking the risk. They warned him nothing of value was inside. But still he persisted.

The prince was determined, some would even say called or compelled, to pursue whatever or whomever was beyond the neglected castle walls. Breaking through the layers and layers of overgrowth covering the castle became his passion.

He climbed for hours and hours, fighting through cobwebs and vines, branches and weeds, until he finally reached the top. As he climbed through the tower window, he saw Sleeping Beauty and was overcome by her beauty. He kissed her and immediately her eyes were opened. She was alive!

 Not only did the princess wake up, but her family woke up, too. And everyone near and dear to her woke up—all because the prince had come for her and claimed her and opened her eyes (and her heart) to what she was missing.

I love how this so mirrors what it's like when Jesus pursues *us*. He loves us. He cares for us. He wants to open our eyes to the beauty around us and to help us best live the life He designed for us.

It's so much goodness—so much love—so much *everything!*—it's hard to fathom, hard to rationalize. Some of us are even tempted to think, 'this is too good to be true!' And it is...*almost*.

As women, we are the primary caregivers for *everyone* and sometimes that makes it hard for us to accept help from others. We care for our spouses, our children, our extended families, our dearest of friends, and even those we don't know so well. It's an instinct Christ planted in our hearts when we were formed; it's part of who we were *divinely designed* to be. That's why it is so important, so crucial, even a matter of life-and-death for the women of this world to be awakened to His calling upon our hearts.

As I continued to learn more and more about the Sleeping Beauty fable, I saw the parallel to Christ's call upon us in so many ways and realized the integral part women— YOU—play in modeling the love of Christ to the many lives we touch. Remember how when she woke up, so did everybody else in the castle? It's the same way in your life, with your spouse, children, and friends. When you become alive in Christ, you can't help but impact others.

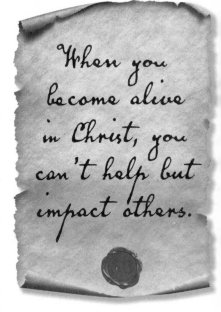

When you become alive in Christ, you can't help but impact others.

Consider your influence on any given day: you rock your babies, you put together a warm meal for your family, you kiss away scraped knees and elbows and a million other things that keep your home running smoothly. And whether you work outside the home or inside, your job description as a wife, mother, and Christ-follower has no boundaries, no set hours, or no coffee breaks. You're on-call 24/7, 365 days a year.

A woman is traditionally the one who brings comfort and care to a home. She makes it inviting and welcoming. And she keeps so many balls in the air at any one time, it's mind blowing.

Soon after my research into the *Sleeping Beauty* story and my revelations about women, I felt the Lord prompting me to search His Word for support. I asked myself, 'Where in The Bible does it talk about all that a woman does and the tremendous influence she has upon others?' I didn't have to look too far for my answer.

In Isaiah 52:1-2, though the Lord is speaking to Israel, His words are also just as applicable to the women of the 21st century. Hear his words:

"Awake, awake, Zion, clothe yourself with strength! Put on your garments of splendor, Jerusalem, the holy city. The uncircumcised and defiled will not enter you again. Shake off your dust;

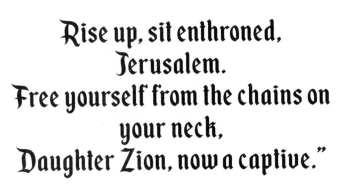

Rise up, sit enthroned, Jerusalem. Free yourself from the chains on your neck, Daughter Zion, now a captive."

Isaiah 52:1-2 (NIV)

Look at the Lord's charge—wake up, get dressed, be strong, break loose. He's telling those held captive to shake the chains that bind them and to begin living boldly. He promises protection and offers freedom. With Christ as our protector, we are free to live a life of boldness and assurance and intention.

We are free to move beyond the mistakes of our past, no matter how grave. We are free to shirk the shame of poor decisions, harmful actions, and hurtful words. We are truly and completely a new and precious creation when we accept the call of our heart to follow Christ in all his ways.

 God wants you to be filled with hope for a better tomorrow and the vision of a life focused on Him.

He knows there will be challenges and difficulties, but He equips you. He knows your heart because he created your heart. And he loves you infinitely more than any of us could begin to grasp. It's a crazy, overwhelming way to live— consistently aware of the Lord's presence in your every days—but it's also *the only way to live* fully awake and fully hopeful.

You have the ability and authority to remove whatever chains that bind you. You are called and you are equipped. Your spirit is called to be one of boldness, not timidity. Nothing you have done or ever will do will be able to separate you from the love of Christ. The past cannot be changed, but the future is one of hope and vision—*Christ's hope and vision for you.*

You are called, dear sister, for great things. These words were meant *for you.*

"Call to me and I will answer you and tell you great and unsearchable things you do not know."

Jeremiah 33:3

This is what God wants us to understand. He will give you the answers to life's most difficult questions. All we have to do is ask.

Kilronan Castle

Ballyfarnon, Co. Roscommon, Ireland

A Visitation from God

One of the revelations that God has given me is that when we get into His presence, *things have to change.*

When we hear holy words from Heaven, everything we see, think, or experience is suddenly filtered through *a holy perspective* because we know it came from God. He allowed or He caused whatever situation we find ourselves in—good, bad, or challenging to be present in our lives. Whether we realize it at the time or not, it's all part of His plan and for His greater glory. When we know and accept this, the change that comes our way can be a *blessed change.*

For so many of us, our lives are filled with demanding schedules. At home and work, church and community, it

seems as if somebody somewhere is always asking something of us. As women of Christ charged with remaining committed to our marriages, raising godly children, and being honorable examples in business and our communities, there's no time clock to punch for our end-of-day responsibilities. We're *always* on duty.

It's exhausting.

And fulfilling.

And it is the call of Christ upon our lives.

And we wouldn't have it any other way.

We live in a world where the noise never stops. NEVER! If you turn off the doom and gloom of the television news, it's still on your laptop or phone. We get updates and notifications. Alerts and warnings. Breaking news and fake news. It comes at us *all day long.* In our family, we sometimes go to great lengths to totally disconnect from all the outside noise. We turn off *everything* that connects us to the outside world, even if only for a brief time.

And you know what happens? The world keeps turning, the events keep happening, and the news cycle keeps going. But we…we get into His presence. We're free of distractions and noise and a million other outside sources jockeying for our attention. We focus on God *and God alone.*

And we are blessed because of it.

Make no mistake, this barrage of media, music, and social media clamor is by design: Satan's design. He wants other things, other people, and other sources of influence to replace the time we spend focusing on God and His provisions for us. Know this, dear sister, if Satan can't make you sin, *he will make you busy.*

It takes a balance of work, play, rest, and prayer to best honor God. If you listen to any (or all!) of the major networks, you'll be filled with nothing more than things of the world; not the things of God. But think about it this way—If you don't spend as much time soaking in God's word as you do the voices of the world, you will be woefully out of balance. And not on the side of God. It all comes down to this:

 If we're not full of God's word, we're full of the world's word.

And that is a recipe for discouragement, depression, and defeat *every time.*

Remember the words Jesus spoke in the Book of Matthew:

"…'Love the Lord your God with all your heart and with all your soul and with all your mind.' This is the first and greatest commandment."

Matthew 22:37-38

Do you hear that and see that, Sleeping Beauty? First and foremost, *above all else,* we are to love the Lord with all that we are—not fill our heads and hearts with the talking heads of the news stations. We were not made to hear every bad thing that is happening around the world every second of every day.

We were made to live from glory to glory!

That's why it is so very important to guard your heart and mind. When you are empty and exhausted, seek the Lord. When you are discouraged and depleted, read the Scriptures. When you don't think you can handle another responsibility at work, make another meal for your family, or settle another family disagreement, press in to find God's presence. He is there; waiting for us to turn and ask for His intercession.

Begin to make declarations over your life. Sing songs of praise and worship at home, in your car, *wherever.* Start a journal of prayers and meditations. It doesn't have to be pages and pages of poetic prayers; it can be one sentence asking for God's intervention. Let your spirit do the 'speaking.' When you enter into the presence and rest of God, you will find peace for a weary heart and quiet from a noisy world.

As I travel around the world, one common theme I hear over and over from women is this:

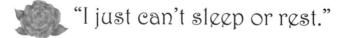

"I just can't sleep or rest."

When we are in a strong hold of fear or anxiety, we can't sleep or rest. It's also when we need a visitation from Jesus the very most. When we recognize the stronghold Satan has upon us, we are called to cast it down, repent, forgive others, and empty out our sins at the feet of the cross. In doing so, we *defeat the devil and accept the victory* of Christ. Hallelujah! It's not always easy, and for most of us, it is a moment-by-moment struggle, but it's also the only real battle worth fighting. And with an assured victory!

Maybe you've heard the old sports saying, "the best offense is a good defense." What that means for us as believers is that, walking closely alongside of The Lord and immersing ourselves in His Scripture is undoubtedly the best offense *for whatever comes our way.* We become armed with The Word and empowered by Christ.

Nehemiah got it right when he told the Levites,

"...'This day is holy to our Lord. Do not grieve, for the joy of the Lord is your strength.'"

Nehemiah 8:10

And again, the words from the Psalms offer the same comfort –

"You make known to me the path of life; you fill me with joy in your presence, with eternal pleasures at your right hand."

Psalm 16:11

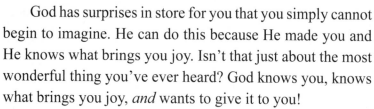

God has surprises in store for you that you simply cannot begin to imagine. He can do this because He made you and He knows what brings you joy. Isn't that just about the most wonderful thing you've ever heard? God knows you, knows what brings you joy, *and* wants to give it to you!

He will set you before your enemies at a banquet and throw a party in your honor. He will celebrate YOU—all that you are to Him and all that He loves about you. Get rid of past hurts and the bitterness of your life and move forward with Christ. He will fight your battles for you and all He asks is that you walk alongside Him.

He wants to take you to a place reserved *just for you*—a place of royal honor. He wants to put a crown on your head and dress you in royal robes just as He did for Queen Esther. He clothed her in royalty outside, but more importantly, He dressed her heart to "prepare her for such a time as this" as she prepared to protect her people.

He wants to do the same for you. Wake up, Sleeping Beauty! This is your time to protect *your* people; your time to influence those around you; your time to *rule and reign.*

Cabra Castle
Kingscourt, Co. Cavan, Ireland

3

I JUST WANT TO BE FREE

have nine *precious* grandchildren and, let me tell you, they each have unique and distinct personalities. Some are always on the go, never-sit-still-for-a-second little ones. A few are quieter and a little more reserved. But *all* of them have me absolutely wrapped around their precious little fingers. My love for each of them runs deep and fierce.

Besides their silly and serious, sad-then-happy personalities, they all have a unique calling upon their young lives. Every once in a while, we'll get a glimpse into the person they may become or the profession they may pursue or the call of their heart. Every day I get to spend with them is an exciting and unpredictable adventure.

I know heaven is glorious, with streets of gold and all that, but being a grandparent has got to be the next best thing this side of meeting Jesus. I'd do without whatever I needed if it meant more for these precious blessings that call me 'Mimi.'

One of my youngest 'blessings' takes closely after her Mimi. She is a spitfire through and through; precocious and energetic in everything she does. We are quite the team when we're together.

When she was somewhere between two- and three-years-old she would occasionally spend the night at our house. We would laugh and play, host tea parties, and read bedtime stories together. Everything would be going along great until around 4 a.m.

Time after time I would be jolted awake by the sweetest, little voice inches away from my face saying, "Mimi, I'm hungry! I want to get up!"

Usually I was so startled I could hardly speak but, the crazy thing is, her daddy—*my son*—used to do the exact same thing so I had had a little practice! Just as I did with him, I would walk Lexie over to the window and say, "Look out the window. Is it still dark outside?"

"Yes," she'd say.

"Okay, so here's the deal—come back and wake me up when the sun comes up!" And off she'd go to play quietly in her room until sunrise.

Not surprisingly, she didn't just get up when she was at

my house. She also got up *and out* at her house—*all the time and when she was still a baby!* At only nine months old, our little firecracker could hoist herself up to the top of the crib and leap out! Nine months!!!

As the saying goes, "Drastic times call for drastic measures" and that's a message her parents took to heart. After doing a little research, we came to realize that apparently sweet Lexie wasn't the only child practicing to become a budding mountaineer and who was routinely leaping from her bed. Who knew there were tents made to fit over baby beds for this exact purpose? Her mom and dad ordered one, we ordered one, anyone who kept Lexie had one.

But that wasn't the end of our adventures. Lexie would scratch and tear at the tent *from the inside* until it was a tattered mess. The whole underneath side was in shreds. Her mom and dad eventually had to put zip ties around the edges to hold the tent in place before Lexie finally conceded. The final score: parents – 1; crafty toddler – 0.

Lexie is lots older now and I asked her not long ago why she was so insistent on getting out of bed. "Mimi," she said, "I just wanted to be free!"

We had a good laugh about her escapades, but her words also struck a chord with me:

 Women of today just want to be free; but there is no real freedom without Jesus.

Jesus came to set us—you and me—free! And to heal our spiritual blindness and open our eyes. And, most importantly, he came to give us life—*an exceedingly abundant* life—now and for all eternity.

Isn't that what we all want? Freedom to simply be. Freedom from judgment; freedom from preconceived notions, freedom from whatever chains the world has placed upon us and even those we've placed upon ourselves. I want freedom, too, but *not just any freedom.* I want The Lord's freedom. I want to be free under the covering of the King of Kings and the Lord of Lords. I want the tremendous security and safety that comes under God's covering, not the kind of freedom I forge for myself.

Throughout my life, I've met many, many women who are not covered by a loving husband or The Lord. As a result, they often do foolish and unwise things. They don't see the value in a covering like Christian women do. They don't realize that a covering is something to be sought and something of value, because it is what ultimately protects us from the snares of Satan. When we get away from God's protection, we open our lives to danger in every form and fashion. Our health is affected, our marriages falter, our children suffer, and our destiny becomes doubtful. But when we turn to The Father, His coverage offers protection in all of these areas.

I know there are so many women of the world intentionally seeking the coverage of The Lord. But for every woman on this path, there are many more on a different, darker, and doomed path. They are following the calling of a dark voice that is urging them to seek freedom—freedom from the provisions and blessings of living a Christ-filled life.

This freedom that these women are so doggedly pursuing has manifested itself in many harmful, destructive, and even deadly ways. Their freedoms mean death for *millions* of unborn babies. Their freedoms allow them to speak with profanities, curse men, live in adulterous or perverse relationships, and to disregard authority. And as if to add insult to injury, these rebels are literally shouting their freedoms in the streets.

The recent decades have brought about unprecedented rebellion in our country and the world. Women have become so consumed with careers, resentful of their families, and covetous of material things, many have crossed over to the dark side of living without God's coverage. It has been a tragic turn of events that seems to be gaining momentum daily. In the past, women have provided so much insight and wisdom and nurturing and love, that in the absence of all this, there is a tremendous void—a void of caring and loving.

When I see the marches of women protesting through the streets, I often wonder, "Do they really know what they're protesting? Do they fully understand the implications of abortion? Or adulterous living? What is it they are really so angry about? Do they care that they are rebelling against The Lord?" My heart breaks when I consider the judgment God may have on these women who openly curse His name and rebel against his sovereignty. I hurt for them and their families because, most assuredly, they will pay a price that will affect their children and even their children's children.

But there's hope, no matter how far they've fallen. The Bible is so wonderfully clear on this point:

> **"...if my people, who are called by my name, will humble themselves and pray and seek my face and turn from their wicked ways, then I will hear from heaven, and I will forgive their sin and will heal their land."**
>
> 2 Chronicles – 7:14

Unless they turn from their wicked ways and repent, their life will be full of shame and tragedy until they draw their last breath on this earth. Those who turn from God and disregard His words will not see the Kingdom of God *and* will face absolute darkness—all for a bit of indulgence during their brief days on earth.

My dear Sleeping Beauty, God wants us to be free. That's why He died for our sins. That's why He wants for us a life of extreme abundance. He came to set us free. He came to break the chains of darkness. He came to cover us in His perfect coverage.

Now is the time for godly women to rise up.

A few months ago, God spoke to me and said, "whatever I have called you to do, you must do, and do it even if you are afraid." I saw a picture with fear on one side and faith on the other. Fear and faith—clearly separated by a line down the middle, were unable to blend together. I've experienced this in real life, too. When I was much younger, I tried to live on both sides and quickly found out it doesn't work. One side always wins out over the other. If you give into fear, you can't remain strong in your faith; likewise, to live a faith-filled life, you have to eventually let go of fear and cross over to the side of faith.

When God called me to live beyond my fear, He promised me this:

"Come and walk on the water with me, yes, the seas will be rolling, the waves crashing, and the wind howling, but on the other side is your destiny."

How could I turn down an offer like this? He was inviting me to come alongside Him, the creator of the world, through whatever came my way, to reach my destiny. Count me in!

He wants the same for you, too. God wants to give you freedom. It's that simple. He wants to open up the windows of heaven to spill out over your life. He wants to fulfill your deepest desires and all He asks of you is to commit to Him. Make your life *His life.*

I feel certain this is a significant time in the history of the world. I see so many women that God is calling upon to rise up and become like modern day Esthers. The voice He has given us is to be used for blessings, not curses. Encouragement, not defeat. Respect, not dishonor.

I speak to women's groups all over the world and one thing I have noticed is that men listen to a woman's voice differently than they do a man's voice—especially a woman's voice that is anointed by the holy hand of God. They know when a woman is under the covering of God and they respond. As women, this means we have a platform to speak a powerful and life-changing message if we keep our hearts pure. It also means we are to use our gifts and callings to spread The Gospel to our hurting world. We can be mighty instruments to fight spiritual warfare here on earth.

Women can also hear things most men cannot. When a newborn in the next room gurgles and coos, women usually hear it. Men may not hear a thing. Most women are just made to be more in tune with the sounds and rhythms of their home and those they love. They can tell when something is not right even by the tone in someone's voice or the look in a loved one's eyes. God created us to be supernaturally fine-tuned.

Women also have an extraordinary sense in the spiritual realm. It's not that they hear more than men, they just hear things on a different frequency than men usually do. We set our spiritual antennae to different wave lengths and that allows us to see things others can't, hear things others can't, and sense things others don't notice. And it all goes back to that's how God created us to be—sensitive, emotionally-connected, and nurturing. By and large, as women, we *feel* what is around us—the mood, the tone, the underlying emotions—and men are traditionally more practical, more pragmatic, and want the clear and concise fact *without* any of the feeling attached. That's what makes men and women the perfect and powerful team. Our perspectives bring balance and insight to the other.

In most households, the responsibility for making sure everyone is well-fed falls upon the woman. It's not that the men can't or won't shop for the groceries and fix the meals; it's just one of the last lines of a traditional household to fall to modern society. And for good reason—it works well this way. Women do well to feed their husbands and children. And that works well whether you're feeding them tacos or prayers.

Before the days of Gerber baby food, the women of ancient civilizations used to chew up their food and then feed it to their babies. It may sound distasteful now, but it was actually a very intentional and selfless act on the mother's part. Instead of receiving the nutritional value of a food, she would take a bite, chew it thoroughly, and give it to her child. She broke down something that was complex and made it pliable and digestible for someone she loved.

Women have been doing this same practice for centuries in spiritual matters, too. I saw this happen week after week when I taught Bible studies at our Shenandoah Ranch. Each week, dozens of ladies would gather to study and pray together. And each week, many of these women's husbands

would wait for their return for them to share what they had learned. The women were taking in the Word of God, digesting it, and feeding it back to the men they loved. Each woman knew the nuances of how her beloved listened to her and each one, in turn, shared what best suited their husbands. Each week we met, it was a blessing to see these women feed upon Scripture and then hear stories of how they shared with their mates.

Girls may be known for 'sugar and spice, and everything nice,' but women can also fight as warriors when necessary. Queen Elizabeth I is a classic example. She became the ruling monarch of Great Britain in 1558 at a time when everything that could go wrong, did go wrong. The country was at war, they were running out of money, running from their enemies, and literally starving. Though daunted, Elizabeth was not without a plan. She rose up and gave a speech and made a declaration to the people—*her people.*

This is a paraphrase of the speech:

"Under God I have my strength. I am willing to live and die among you. In the midst and heat of battle I will fight for my country, my people, and my God. I will take up my sword and fight. I know I have the body of a weak, feeble woman, but inside I have the heart of a King."

When I read this, I began to cry because *her heart was my heart.* She knew (and readily conceded) that she didn't have the physical strength and stamina of a man, but she did have the strength of conviction to lead her people and an unshakeable faith to depend upon. Haven't you ever felt that way, too? It's like the weight of the world is on your shoulders sometimes. But as a believer, you eventually realize you're not carrying the load alone; the Lord has come alongside to ease your burdens and give you rest and comfort.

I know so many women who work both inside and outside their home—basically holding down two full-time jobs. As women, we make decisions all day long—like a king, but in a softer package. It's a huge responsibility that can sometimes have many long-term repercussions. Though we be tender and beautiful on the outside, women can undoubtedly handle warfare when necessary. Pretty and fierce *can* coexist in a single package; women prove it every day.

I practice warfare of the spiritual kind every day for my family, my community, and those around the world. And believe me, my kind of warfare produces some amazing results. There have been many nights when I have quietly tiptoed out of my room and into my prayer closet for a few more minutes with God. When the storms of life have come upon my family, I have learned to hit my knees in prayer and to stay there until I know my prayers and pleas are heard and heaven has reached earth.

It is our privilege as women to listen to the people around us and to hear—*really hear*—what is being said and to intercede on behalf of those who depend upon us. We have been given this spirit of discernment to comfort

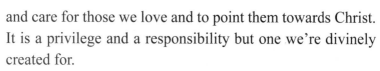

and care for those we love and to point them towards Christ. It is a privilege and a responsibility but one we're divinely created for.

I am challenging you, Sleeping Beauty, to stand up.

Rise up and wise up and fight for your family. Your nation. Your God. And do it in a way that pleases God.

You have been given a powerful voice; use it to bring glory to God.

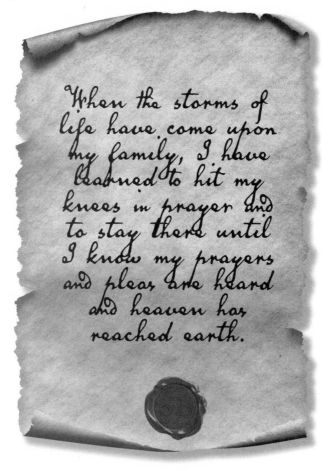

When the storms of life have come upon my family, I have learned to hit my knees in prayer and to stay there until I know my prayers and pleas are heard and heaven has reached earth.

Ballyseede Castle

Tralee, Co. Kerry, Ireland

WOMEN OF THE BIBLE
WHO WOKE UP

We all have a standing invitation to wake up to God's calling. And when we do decide to follow Christ, adjustments have to be made. The moment you accept Christ's calling upon your life, you step into holy obedience. I believe all of heaven opens up over our lives when we choose to follow the good and perfect plan God has designed especially for us.

The Lord promises to go before you, alongside of you, and behind you to protect you. He made this promise to the Israelites as they were crossing out of Egypt and He makes it for us, too:

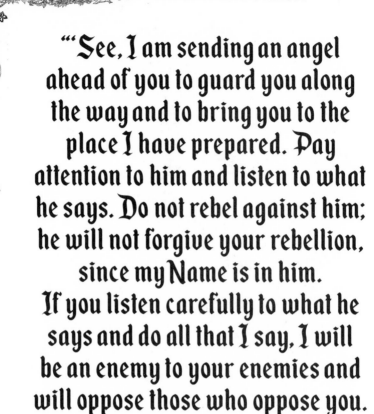

"'See, I am sending an angel ahead of you to guard you along the way and to bring you to the place I have prepared. Pay attention to him and listen to what he says. Do not rebel against him; he will not forgive your rebellion, since my Name is in him. If you listen carefully to what he says and do all that I say, I will be an enemy to your enemies and will oppose those who oppose you. My angel will go ahead of you...'"

Exodus 23:20-23

Just as He provided angels to cover and protect His chosen people more than 2,000 years ago, He still offers us angels to keep us safe and give us guidance.

The Bible also gives us guidance and encouragement through the stories of women who rose up and made a difference for their families and their people. Some of these women were stellar examples from the start, but many of them were anything but positive role models before committing to follow Christ.

Deborah was a powerful woman of tremendous influence in Israel in 1200 BC—*especially for a woman.* In the Book of Judges, we are told she was a prophetess, counselor, warrior, and judge. In fact, she was the only woman judge in all of Israel. She was multi-tasking long before it was cool! She was married to a man named Lappidoth. I can't help but think Lappidoth must have been some kind of secure and confident gentleman to have been married to such an accomplished woman and not be intimidated by her power!

As a judge, Deborah would sit daily under a date palm tree and render her judgments to the people. When she had finally had enough of the wretched condition of the people of Israel, she sent for Barak, a general in the army. She told him the time had come for Israel to fight. She also told him to ready 10,000 men for battle and that she would deliver his enemies directly in his path.

Unbelievably, Barak agreed to go, but on one condition: if she would go with him; otherwise he refused to lead his men into battle. Deborah agreed, but she had conditions of her own as well: "'Certainly I will go with you,' said Deborah. 'But because of the course you are taking, the honor will not be yours, for the Lord will deliver Sisera (the enemy) into the hands of a woman.'" (Judges 4:9).

Deborah clearly knew how to call the shots and lead her people.

She ultimately gave the order telling Barak and his army when they were to advance and The Lord routed their enemies directly towards them, setting them up for a certain defeat. When the battle ended, the only survivor was their leader, Sisera, who had escaped on foot. Thinking he was safe, he fled to the tent of a woman named Jael, whom he

considered safe. Knowing who he was, Jael put him at ease by offering him something to drink and a blanket for rest. When he accepted her offers and fell asleep, she took advantage of his vulnerable position and drove a tent peg through his temple and killed him.

Not long after, Barak arrived on the scene. Jael was proud of her part in helping Israel become victorious and went out to greet him. "'Come,' she said, 'I will show you the man you're looking for.'" (Judges 4:22).

These were two significant victories for the people of Israel—defeating the huge army of Sisera and killing their leader. Even more significant is that these victories happened because two brave and obedient women, who were attuned to the words and directions of Christ, helped their countrymen defeat thousands of warriors and their escaped leader. Deborah, in particular, prophesied that the enemy would be defeated and her army victorious. In celebration of her prophesy being realized, she even wrote a lengthy song in Judges 5 that tells of her country's victory. The final verse pretty much sums up her gratitude to the Lord for His intervention:

> **"'So, may all your enemies
> perish, Lord!
> But may all who love you
> be like the sun
> When it rises in its strength.'"**
>
> Judges 5:31

I would like to think there are many godly women who are ready to fight for their families, children, cities, and nations. If each of us could only wake up and use our God-given authority to call down heaven's power, *all of our battles* could be won.

I know many women who have the word of the Lord in their hearts. It is evident in how they speak and act and think. They take to heart the words of Scripture and live it out. The world needs more of these women to use their voice and their wisdom to make a difference in the world and to live as godly examples for women everywhere. I don't think it's an exaggeration to say the future of our families, communities, and country depends upon it.

Another example of a woman who woke from a spiritual sleep was the Samaritan woman who met Jesus at the well. From the start of His travels, Jesus' disciples had tried to talk Him out of even going through Samaria on His way from Judea to Galilee. The country was known to be the home of criminals and social outcasts and had a reputation as a troublesome country, but Jesus persisted.

When He became weary and thirsty, He stopped alongside a water well. When a Samaritan woman approached, he asked her for a drink. This was unconventional and even scandalous in so many ways. First, Jews did not associate with Samaritans; second, a Jewish *man* speaking to a Samaritan *woman in public* was all sorts of wrong in those days. The woman was so taken aback, she replied, "How can you ask me for a drink?" (John 4:9).

This is how the story goes from there:

"Jesus answered her, 'If you knew the gift of God and who it is that asks you for a drink, you would have asked him and he would have given you living water.'

'Sir,' the woman said, 'you have nothing to draw with and the well is deep. Where can you get this living water?...'

Jesus answered, 'Everyone who drinks this water will be thirsty again, but whoever drinks the water I give them will never thirst. Indeed, the water I give them will become in them a spring of water welling up to eternal life.'

The woman said to him, 'Sir, give me this water so that I won't get thirsty and have to keep coming here to get water.'

He told her, 'Go, call your husband and come back.'

'I have no husband,' she replied.

Jesus said to her, 'You are right when you say you have no husband. The fact is, you have had five husbands, and the man you now have is not your husband. What you have just said is quite true.'

'Sir,' the woman said, 'I can see that you are a prophet...'"

From there, Jesus went on to explain that a time was coming when true worshippers would worship the Father in Spirit and in truth.

The woman said, "I know that Messiah (called Christ) is coming. When he comes, he will explain everything to us."

Then Jesus declared, "I, the one speaking to you—I am he." (John 4:10-11, 13-19, 25-26).

Right there, in the hot desert sun, with no one else around, a Samaritan woman—had an encounter with the one, true living God. And her life was changed in an instant

She could hardly contain herself when she realized she was standing in the presence of God. She was so excited, she left her water jar and ran back to her town exclaiming, "'Come, see a man who told me everything I ever did. Could this be the Messiah?' (John 4:29).

She knew she was in the presence of holiness. She knew her life had been forever changed. And she knew she wanted the people of her town to share in her joy and conviction and conversion. Little doubt, this Samaritan woman was the first female evangelist in her country.

Can you begin to imagine coming face-to-face with Jesus when you're in the middle of an everyday, mundane, 'have-to' task? Like in the school carpool line or at the grocery store or folding laundry. One minute you're just tending to the details of everyday living; the next you've been completely transformed and are a child of God. What a glorious day it must have been for this dirty and dejected woman to be awakened by the Savior.

After having been married five times, this woman had almost assuredly given up on the hope of another, permanent relationship with a man who could love her and care for her. Although she had most likely lost her husbands through famine or war, she probably could never have imagined that someone could see past her life of sin and hopelessness and actually love her *for her.*

Yet she was exactly the kind of person Christ came to earth for.

In the blink of an eye, this woman of shame and poverty became a daughter of a king—*The King!* Her past was forgiven and forgotten and her future was assured. She was now an evangelist and an ambassador of Christ charged with telling everyone she met about Him.

The Samaritan woman isn't an exception; *she's the norm.* She was asleep in her sin, she encountered Christ, and immediately she was awakened to her calling and destiny. We may not still be drawing water from wells these days, but we're just as likely to meet Christ throughout our days, too, and be awakened to His calling.

One more story of a Sleeping Beauty awakened by Christ is told in the Book of John about the woman accused of adultery. Jesus is teaching and preaching in the temple when the Pharisees bring a woman caught in the middle of adultery and make her stand in front of the group. "'Teacher, this woman was caught in the act of adultery. In the Law Moses commanded us to stone such women. Now what do you say?'" (John 8:4-5).

With that, Jesus knelt to the ground and began writing in the dirt as if He didn't hear them. In my heart, I believe He was writing the names of her accusers who were sinners, but we don't know that for sure. When they kept questioning Him, Jesus straightened back up and said, "'Let any one of you who are without sin to be the first to throw a stone at her.'" (John 8:7).

And then He knelt again and continued to write as the accusers walked away one by one.

I can imagine Jesus looking at this distraught, accused, and forsaken woman straight in the eye as she stood alone in the dirt, accused, caught, and guilty of a sin punishable by death. Think about how amazing it was for her in that moment when the Savior of the world knelt down in the dirt alongside of her and turned the spotlight of conviction upon her accusers. Jesus—*God in the flesh!*—kneeling and comforting a broken and defeated woman in front of so many self-righteous men. My heart is so moved when I think of the marvelous, overwhelming love that my heavenly father has for me and for the women of this world. How could we ever consider resisting such love? This is *exactly* what we long for—to be loved for who we are, as we are, unconditionally.

As the story continues, the woman's accusers left one at a time until none remained. Jesus straightened up and asked her, "'Woman, where are they? Did no one condemn you?'

She said, 'No, one, Lord.'

And Jesus said, 'I do not condemn you, either. Go. From now on sin no more.'" (John 8:10-11 NASB).

She knew she was standing in the presence of Christ because she called him Lord. The spiritual eyes of this Sleeping Beauty had been opened. She had met her master and she was living proof of Isaiah's promise:

"'Though your sins are like scarlet, they shall be as white as snow;...'"

Isaiah 1:18

This adulterous woman—literally caught in her sin—was forgiven by the One, True, Living Christ, and her life would never be the same afterward.

Fast forward 2,000+ years to a lesson I learned about carrying unnecessary guilt and burdens, much like the woman caught in adultery experienced. I am married to what many people refer to as 'the most interesting man in the world.' And for good reason, too! He has backpacked in the French Alps, hiked the Inca Trail in Peru, climbed

Mount Kilimanjaro, dogsledded in the fjords of Norway, and traveled down the Amazon River—just to name a few of his extraordinary experiences.

Several years ago, while he and a group of friends were hiking a particularly high mountain in France, one of the guys, Rainey, started putting rocks in his buddy's backpack unbeknownst to him. Rainey is known far and wide as a practical joker and is always looking for ways to pull a trick on someone. On this day, Richard was a on the receiving end of Rainey's pranks.

Every time the group stopped to rest, Rainey would somehow slip a few extra rocks into Richard's backpack, adding more and more weight as the guys went higher and higher. Before too long, Richard started feeling almost too tired to go on, yet all his buddies seemed to be taking the trail without too much effort. Mind you, these guys are all in great shape and have climbed mountains as high as 19,000+ feet, but today, Richard was lagging behind everyone and growing more tired along the way.

When the team finally reached the summit, Richard about collapsed and said, "This mountain is kicking my booty. It is weighing me down so much I don't know if I can go on any further." And that's when the rest of the crew burst out laughing and Rainey came clean about his rock-upon-rock rest stop escapades. Needless to say, Richard was relieved that he really wasn't that out of shape and that he'd been carrying LOTS of extra weight that he didn't need to and the others hadn't been carrying.

I laughed so hard when the guys told the story about Richard and Rainey and their mountaintop adventures, but I also heard a whisper in my spirit, too. It spoke to my soul when it said, "that's what the world does to you, too." From morning till evening, in conversations big and small, from the words and images of television, the movies, and magazines, this is exactly what the world does to us:

It places unnecessary expectations and demands on our lives, and negative, destructive, even violent, words and images on the hard-drive of our hearts and minds and souls.

When we let negative words, broken relationships, spoken curses, financial pressures, sickness, mental and emotional stress, and the news of the day speak into our lives, it is as if we are depositing unnecessary rocks into our backpack of life. We are carrying well beyond what we are designed to carry. It is time to empty your backpack of worries, anxieties, and fears and to free our minds of all that isn't Christ. God does not want for us to carry these burdens; that is His job. The soothing words of the Psalms tell us specifically to release these burdens:

"Cast your cares on the Lord and he will sustain you; he will never let the righteous be shaken."

Psalm 55:22

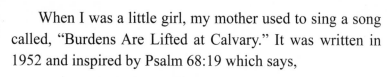

When I was a little girl, my mother used to sing a song called, "Burdens Are Lifted at Calvary." It was written in 1952 and inspired by Psalm 68:19 which says,

"Praise be to the Lord, to God our Savior, who daily bears our burdens."

Psalm 68:19

The lyrics go like this:

> Days are filled with sorrow and care,
> Hearts are lonely and drear;
> Burdens are lifted at Calvary,
> Jesus is very near.

> Cast your care on Jesus today,
> Leave your worry and fear;
> Burdens are lifted at Calvary,
> Jesus is very near.

> Troubled soul, the Savior can see every
>   heartache and tear;
> Burdens are lifted at Calvary,
> Jesus is very near.

And the refrain:
Burdens are lifted at Calvary,
Calvary, Calvary;
Burdens are lifted at Calvary,
Jesus is very near.

Whenever I would hear my mother sing these words, the notes would echo through the house and so would a feeling of peace. Today, when I hear this melody and sing these words, I still feel that same peace. It's as if these words help me to unpack the worry, anxiety, and concerns of my life. I hear The Lord speak to me and say, "Cast your care on me, your burdens are lifted at Calvary, Jesus is very near."

Wherever you are in your spiritual walk, take a minute to close your eyes and lift up your hands in surrender. Raise them to heaven and ask Jesus to take the 'rocks' from your backpack, to lift you up, and to renew your strength. He knows what lies ahead tomorrow, next week, and next year and wants us to give it all to Him. He is listening to our cries for help and direction and He wants to overshadow us with His peace. When we lay our burdens and disappointments, frustrations and feelings, at His feet, He will pick them up and carry them for us.

Leave the rocks behind and lighten your load; Christ will carry whatever you leave behind.

Dromoland Castle

Newmarket-on-Fergus, Co. Clare, Ireland

5

MODERN DAY
SLEEPING BEAUTIES

A few years ago, I was invited to a "Revive Your Heart Conference" led by Nancy DeMoss Wolgemuth in Indianapolis. It was a great conference all around—terrific speakers, fun and interesting presentations, and lots of wonderful fellowship with other Christian women. I still remember so many things from that wonderful gathering, but for me, one speaker stood out from the rest and her story still resonates with me today.

Her name is Chrissy Cymbala and she is a modern day Sleeping Beauty.

Chrissy is the daughter of Jim and Carol Cymbala, pastors of the world-renown Brooklyn Tabernacle Church

in New York. She was raised learning and growing in the Lord, but she was also surrounded by the rough and tumble streetwise kids of the area. She was covered in prayer by her parents and many of the church, but the constant exposure to so much darkness around her eventually gained a foothold in her life.

Although she played the piano, sang in the church choir, and worshipped every Sunday with her family, somewhere along the way she became deceived and fell into an ungodly relationship and became completely estranged from God. Before long, she began sneaking out of the house to spend time with her boyfriend and then would make up lies to cover her deceit. Her parents thought she was back on the right path when she left for a Bible college, but that didn't last long when she was kicked out of the school. Even though she returned to home and her family, she still remained lost and rebellious.

When she became pregnant, she left home—with no place to go. Her parents banned her from their home unless she made some significant changes to her life. Even though her dad, a world-famous pastor, considered himself to be a good father, he felt as if God would not release him to bring her home until she repented and quit making a lie out of her Christianity. To her credit, Chrissy tried many times to break away from this ungodly relationship, but she simply never could. She was in the pit of sin and simply couldn't get out.

At one of her lowest points, Chrissy called a woman she knew from church and begged the woman to allow her and her newborn baby to stay with her for a few days. The woman called Pastor Cymbala and asked for his input.

"It's your decision," he told the lady, "I cannot do anything for her because God has not released me to bring her home."

Throughout this time, the 16,000-member church continued to have powerful prayer meetings every Tuesday evening. Pastor Cymbala couldn't bring himself to ask for special prayers for Chrissy because he thought it too selfish in the midst of all the drugs and destruction, even death, that literally surrounded the church and its neighborhood. Eventually, someone brought a note asking to pray for Chrissy and her father finally agreed.

He got up in front of the many gathered for the prayer meeting and told them Chrissy was lost and away from God. He told them their family had been praying for quite some time, but that he hadn't told his congregation just how lost she was. But finally—*that evening*—was to become her night of deliverance.

The people that were at the prayer meeting that night said it felt as if heaven touched the earth as so many prayed on behalf of Chrissy. The people wept and wailed for her and her child to return to Christ and the church. Several thousand people stormed the gates of heaven with heartfelt pleas on behalf of the whole Cymbala family. Their cry was for this wayward daughter, their pastor's precious child *and her child*, to repent and come home. They wanted this prodigal child—*their* prodigal child—to return to the God she had forsaken and to shake free of the chains that bound her.

On this night, the woman Chrissy had been staying with went to the prayer meeting and Chrissy and the baby stayed home *alone*. While lying in her bed, Chrissy felt something enter her room. She said it was the most disgusting, hideous creature (or spirit) she had ever seen—almost like a swirling flame of evil.

On the other side of her bed, Chrissy remembers seeing a picture of light and beauty, full of life and warmth. Chrissy saw the evil creature moving towards her baby's crib and heard him say, "I have her; now I am going to have her baby."

Normally most of us, Chrissy included, would have been filled with fear and screamed in terror if we were to see such a monster—especially if it moved near our children. But for some reason, fear eluded her that night. Instead, she closed her eyes and fell asleep.

The next morning, Chrissy awoke feeling light and free. She even called to the woman she was staying with and asked her to pray with her. They joined hands and Chrissy prayed, "Lord, let me say goodbye to this relationship. Set me free! In Jesus' name, Amen." And that was the turning point in her life. And her baby's life. And her family's life. One simple, 'HELP,' shouted to the heavens, and provision and intercession were delivered. The chains were broken and held her no more. She was finally free!

She called her boyfriend and told him the relationship was over. Even though she had tried many times before, she said this time was different. This time she was breaking free and the relationship was finally over.

The next day Chrissy borrowed a car and drove to her parent's home. She had done this several times before, but her father would not agree to meet with her. But this time… *this time,* when she knocked on the door, her dad came running down the stairs to welcome his child and *her child* into his arms, his home, and his heart.

When she shares her testimony, Chrissy tells how sin had worked a number on her life. Sin upon sin led her to continually feel beat down, exhausted, and hopeless. She was literally down and out and without any sort of back-up plan. But when she crossed the threshold of her family home, she knew she was *free*. She also shares how she fell on her knees and lifted her hands toward heaven as soon as she got inside.

"Mom and Dad," she said, "I repent. Jesus, I repent! Left to me I would destroy my life, but Jesus forgave me. My cravings are sinful. I am turning everything over to Jesus. *I repent!"*

Chrissy shares how her dad lifted her up *and* his precious, new granddaughter and said, "This Sunday, we are going to dedicate my precious granddaughter to the Lord in front of the whole church and my daughter is finally coming home!" Sure enough, the church was packed to celebrate this prodigal daughter's return to the God she knew as a child and the family that loved her so deeply.

Let this story be encouraging and hopeful if you are the parent (or grandparent) of a wayward child. Don't *ever* give up on their future and praying for their return. God is listening to the cries of our hearts. And we never know which prayer it is that tilts the scales of heaven in our favor. God wants you to pray, pray, and keep praying and not give up until your child comes home.

And if you're more like Chrissy than her parents, learn from her path. If you're in a bad relationship, break it off *today.* Do not spend your days in sin and depression. You are worth so much more. God wants to give you beauty from the ashes of your mess. He wants to fill you with His Spirit and bring you home. His words from Jeremiah are proof of His provisions for us:

> ## "'For I know the plans I have for you,'" declares the Lord, 'plans to prosper you and not to harm you, plans to give you hope and a future.'"

Jeremiah 29:11

Our hopes, our dreams, *our plans*—all are secure when we cling to the promises of our Lord—even when we wander far, far away. Your plans are secure, Sleeping Beauty. Awake and be hopeful!

Trim Castle

Trim, Co. Meath, Ireland

GOD'S PLAN TO WAKE UP
THE SLEEPING BEAUTIES

Some people are what most of us call 'morning people'—they're up with the sun and ready to get on about the business of their day. Others of us are considerably more nocturnal and seem to hit our sweet spot later in the evening—*much later!* I am most definitely the later one.

If I have a project that needs to get done, I know I do my best work late into the night, singing away well into the wee hours of the morning. Even when I don't have projects to wrap up or events to prepare for, I still love the quiet and peace of late night when I have no pressing agenda to attend to, the house is quiet, and I have the sweet blessing of hours ahead of me to do as I wish.

My husband is exactly the opposite. *The complete opposite.* He wakes up happy and energized and ready to greet the day. For him, the morning is his *prime time* when he's rarin' to get going and get things done. I kid him that he's so happy to be 'up and at it' for a new day, that sometimes he sounds like Andrea Bocelli, the world-famous opera singer, in the shower. The man loves his mornings.

After many, many years of marriage, we know some of our tendencies are here to stay and there's no use trying to change what comes naturally for each of us. This means he will probably always be a morning person and I, most definitely, will probably always *not* be a morning person. It's just one of many differences that we accept and appreciate about one another.

Let me give you an example of how this plays out in our relationship: We have a home high in the mountains in Colorado, more than 9,000 feet above sea level. It's one of my most favorite places in the entire world. When we're there and there's foot upon foot of fresh snow on the ground, there is no place I'd rather be than snuggled up in a cozy bed with lots of feather pillows and a silky down comforter to keep me warm. It's heaven on earth and I could spend hours tucked in my little cocoon while admiring the snowdrifts *outside.*

My husband loves these days just as much as I do, but for a different reason. He wants to go hiking! He wants to see the fresh snow firsthand and see the tracks made from animals the night before. He wants to take in the stillness and quiet of the morning when everything is blanketed in white. He wants to bundle up, get at it, and hike like we're old-timey explorers discovering new things.

Because I love him so, I'm usually game to go on his early-a.m. expeditions and because he loves me so, he knows the way to encourage me to lace up my hiking boots starts slowly and with coffee. And fresh cream.

On these mornings, he has learned the best way to win me over is with a cup of freshly brewed hot coffee. If you love coffee as much as I do, you can appreciate that mornings with coffee always start better than those without. I can be sound asleep but when he tiptoes in and sets a cup of hot coffee with fresh cream by my bedside, I can't help but wake up to that sweet aroma. I simply can't resist such a wonderful wake-up call.

In my studies of God and how he works so decidedly in the lives of women, I've come to realize that God uses all sorts of different ways to wake us up because we all respond to different types of wake-up calls. What wakes me up may not even phase you; and what stirs you might not do the trick for me. The Lord knows that because he created us to be attuned and sensitive to different things.

When we are awakened, we're called to return to consciousness. That might mean we're roused, excited, provoked, alerted or spurred to action. It can also mean to call forth or to breathe life into someone or something. It's no small thing to be awakened. Lots of wheels are set in motion when we are awakened.

For so many years, generations of women have been asleep, slumbering in someone else's reality. We're captivated by the seemingly perfect lives of movie stars and entertainers. All we see is the glitz and glamour of their lives and compare it to the dirty dishes, piles of laundry, and kids that won't nap in our own lives. They appear to have

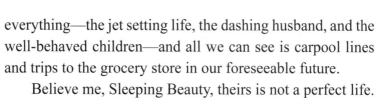

everything—the jet setting life, the dashing husband, and the well-behaved children—and all we can see is carpool lines and trips to the grocery store in our foreseeable future.

Believe me, Sleeping Beauty, theirs is not a perfect life. Nor is the life of the mom at school who always seems to have it all together. Or the always-waving neighbor down the street. But you, precious, precious Sleeping Beauty have what many of these women don't—and that is a unique calling upon your life to be His—to live as a chosen bride, to share his words with everyone you touch, and to be an ambassador for His Kingdom in your sphere of influence.

God's dream and destiny for you cannot be compared with any movie star, pop singer, or royal queen on the planet. Literally, *no one else on the entire planet.* He has placed within you a specific design with desires deep within your heart that only a relationship with our Father, Abba God, can fulfill. Isn't that overwhelming when you think about it? The God of the universe sought you out, claimed you as His own, and fashioned within you a one-of-a-kind heart and soul that sets you apart from everyone else in the world.

You have an eternal call upon your life. DON'T MISS IT! Don't try to copy how someone else answers *their* calling; answer *your* calling. Don't clutter your mind with the competitions of trying to be like others; fill it with the words of Scripture. Ask the Lord to direct *you* as you pursue your calling and He will faithfully respond. Let Him awaken you to His divine plan for your life.

One of my favorite scriptures is found in Psalms:

"Take delight in the Lord, and He will give you the desires of your heart."

Psalm 37:4

For so many of us, we sometimes don't even know what desires we have until we find The One who connects us with our purpose. We don't even know *what* we want until we know *who* wants us. And then…then it is as if all the dots are connected and we become fully awake—energized and full of passion for whatever it is that God has put within our heart. And that, dear sister, is a beautiful place to be.

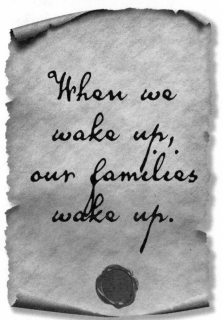

When we wake up, our families wake up.

As women, we are powerful. *Very* powerful. We have so much influence over what happens in the world, how it happens, and why it happens. Sometimes we're seen and recognized for our obvious influence; other times it is more subtle and less evident, but it is *always* present. That's why it is so important to become fully awake—because our influence has the potential to be far and wide. When we wake up, our families wake up. And when we are roused and challenged, we set the example for so many around us. It is not an exaggeration

to say that women who know and embrace who they are in Christ have the power to wake an entire nation.

Esther is a great example of a woman who became alive in Christ and saved her entire kingdom in the process. There's little doubt that the enemy has been trying to destroy the power and influence of women from the beginning of time, but God knew otherwise. As far back as the first book in the Bible, God said to the first woman, Eve, "you will strike his heel" (Genesis 3:15), meaning she (and all women afterward) would have dominion over Satan. As women, we are empowered to overcome Satan when we put our minds to it. When we are attuned to God's unique calling upon our own lives, Satan doesn't stand a chance.

A woman walking in step with her Savior can overcome anything.

As much as I like to take my time waking up, not everyone has it so gently. That is certainly the case for members of the Corps of Cadets at Texas A&M University. Though the college is largely civilian students, the 2,000-member Corps plays a vital role in maintaining the school's hallowed traditions. One of these is the call to regular morning formation and drills that occurs when reveille is sounded on the bugle. Every school day, a bugler stands at attention and breaks the early morning silence with the loud and clear call of reveille.

I was curious where the word 'reveille' comes from and did a little research to find out how it came to be associated with a young cadet and his bugle. Interestingly, the word 'reveille' comes from the French word, 'reveil,' which appropriately means to wake up. For centuries, the call of reveille has been used to wake up and call to action military personnel and prisoners in correctional institutions. I think the simplicity of the call is what makes it so effective: it's loud, it's clear, it overshadows any other noise, and it is unmistakable in its call to awaken. It's a call to action for soldiers to face the day and fight the battle to which they are called.

And it's just as relevant for women—the defenders of and fighters for our homes and families—to face the day before us and answer the call to which we have each been called. Trust me on this: God is calling us to our call of duty. It is time to brush off our uniforms, whether they be designer dresses or yoga pants, and to assume our place of authority to love and lead our families as Christ would. Our assignments are ready; it is up to each of us to prepare for the battle that faces our homes, our husbands, our children, and our communities every day. When we neglect the call to action, we give Satan another foothold into the hearts and minds of those we love most.

Besides calling soldiers and fighters to battle, reveille was also called to awaken prisoners—those traditionally convicted of a crime and held against their will for the protection of society. Ironically, that's much like it is in dealings with the Evil One because, when Satan goes unchecked, we become condemned as prisoners of sin and are held against our will.

But that is not how God designed us to live. He wants us in bondage to no one. He wants freedom for our hearts, minds, and souls. He wants us to realize the freedom a life spent with Him will provide.

When I first heard the word of the Lord and his call to use me to awaken the Sleeping Beauties of the world, he opened my eyes to these words of Isaiah:

> "Wake up, wake up, O Zion!
> Clothe yourself with strength.
> Put on your beautiful clothes, O
> holy city of Jerusalem,
> for unclean and godless people
> will enter your gates no longer.
> Rise from the dust, O Jerusalem.
> Sit in a place of honor.
> Remove the chains of slavery
> from your neck,
> O captive daughter of Zion.
> For this is what the Lord says:
> 'When I sold you into exile,
> I received no payment.
> Now I can redeem you,
> without having to pay for you.'"

Isaiah 52:1-3 (NLT)

As you study the commentary on this scripture, you can see that God is calling his people—his daughters of Zion—

to be summoned to the highest glory possible. He is telling them to put on their garments of beauty and to be lifted to the dignity that is theirs as his followers. They are told to loosen the cords of slavery and embrace the freedom that awaits them.

More than two centuries later, we are still being called to freedom. The words first spoken to the Israelites are meant for us, too. Just like them, we are to free ourselves from the ties that bind us and accept the freedom Christ extends to each of us. We are no longer to be prisoners or slaves; our freedom has been secured.

When I think of what this looks like in terms of pictures, I see a woman groveling in the dirt. She's ashamed and broken, held captive by what she thinks are unforgivable sins. But then, I see the Father God charging toward her on a white horse and leading an army of angel warriors. Suddenly He shouts to her, "You are free, take the cords off your neck; the chains are already broken! Get up, O daughter of Zion! I have come to take you to a place you have never been to and show you things you have never seen. I have come to give you life abundantly."

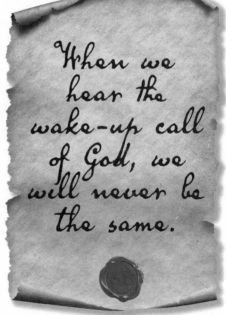

When we hear the wake-up call of God, we will never be the same.

When we hear the wake-up call of God, we will never be the same. *Ever.* No experience on earth can compare to what happens when a

woman realizes the call of God upon her life. Everything—every single thing—changes the moment we say "yes" to the Father. From my own experience, I can tell you that when you yield to the call and truly fall in love with the Savior, your life will forever be different. The prophet Jeremiah spoke of this, too:

> ## "This is what the Lord says, ... 'Call to me and I will answer you and tell you great and unsearchable things you do not know.'"
>
> Jeremiah 33:2-3

When we are truly awake and keenly aware of God's voice, He begins showing us bit by bit glimpses of our future with Him. We take on a heavenly perspective and realize what awaits us is far better than anything here on earth. No Hollywood movie set or royal palace can hold a candle to what God has planned for each of us when we fully submit to His plans for each of us.

For me, the glimpses of God's presence in my life frequently come as surprises. I intentionally ask God for good surprises and He has blessed me more times than I can count. I love the excitement and adventure of a wonderful, unexpected blessing, especially those that happen with no explanation or that can't be orchestrated to happen. Believe me when I tell you that you can experience these same sweet reminders of God's presence in your daily life, too. When you give your heart to God, He will amaze you with a life full of passion and purpose.

And probably a few heaven-sent surprises, too.

Throughout my studies of Christ's calling upon our lives and how He works to snag our attention, I have found three primary ways we are awakened. The first way He speaks to us is by convicting us in our hearts. God knows when we are in rebellion and when we are, He begins to speak to us and deal with our conscience. We all know that unsettled feeling when we know we've done something wrong or disappointed someone. When it is the Lord we've offended with our thoughts and words and actions, the feelings are intensified. We toss and turn, usually unable to sleep. Our spirit is troubled to the point of hopelessness when we become overwhelmed with the conviction of sin.

But we are by no means hopeless. In fact, we should be the most hope*ful* people ever. That is because God stands by, ever ready to help us wake up to the sin in our lives, and ever willing to lead the way *towards Him*. Scripture tells each of us He directs us in all our doubts and difficulties and comforts us in times of fear and distress. I like to imagine Scripture as if it were a bright torch on a dark, dark night, leading the way to prevent us from stumbling over obstacles, falling into traps, and veering off His intended path for us. When we follow the path He sets before us, honor His correction, and heed the warning signs of impending danger, we are at our safest. The promise of Psalm 119:105 captures this word-picture perfectly:

"Your word is a lamp for my feet, a light on my path."

Psalm 119:105

If the conviction in our hearts isn't enough to cause us to wake up to God's calling, He oftentimes sends a friend or a prophet to speak to us. It might not even be a direct conversation but word of scripture you see somewhere or a message from church or elsewhere. However, it comes to you, you know when you hear it that it's from the Lord and he's seeking to gain your attention.

In 2 Samuel, the prophet Nathan was sent to King David to tell him a parable of a man who stole a sheep from a man who had little else. When King David heard of this injustice, he said, "As surely as the Lord lives, the man who did this must die! He must pay for that lamb four times over, because he did such a thing and had no pity." Then Nathan said to David, "You are the man!...(2 Samuel 12:5-7). Nathan said this because he knew David had committed adultery with another man's wife and then had her husband killed. Nathan was sent to

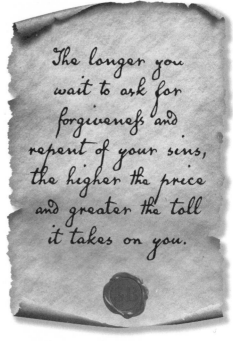

The longer you wait to ask for forgiveness and repent of your sins, the higher the price and greater the toll it takes on you.

help David see his sin and his great need to repent for all that he had done. The message worked: David did repent but lost his son and endured much family tragedy throughout the rest of his reign as king.

There is nothing so grave that the Lord can't forgive, but don't take His grace and mercy lightly. The longer you wait to ask for forgiveness and repent of your sins, the higher the price and greater the toll it takes on you. God will do whatever is necessary to open your eyes to your sinful nature. The quicker you accept this and His outstretched hand of forgiveness, the less strife and turmoil you'll endure. This doesn't mean your life will be free from problems—even some big, life-altering challenges—but it does mean you'll find comfort in the hollow of His holy hand and be given a peace that defies explanation.

This leads us to the final, and most drastic, measure God will use to wake you from your destructive life path: a hardship aimed at helping you see the intense need for His presence in your life. You can be operating as if you have everything under control and see little need to walk in tandem with a savior. You think you can do it all, control everything, and keep all of life's balls in the air. And you usually can…for a while. That is, until the protective hedge and blessing are lifted from your life.

You might not even notice it at first. Maybe you no longer hear the Lord's voice or sense the Holy Spirit's presence; maybe you begin to feel restless, even unable to sleep. Before long, you begin to feel alone even if you're surrounded by others. That's because you have come to understand that life without God truly is hopeless.

This wake-up call is, by far, the most dangerous because, by this point, you have become your own god. *You* are the standard against which you judge everything; you are the one who sets your moral compass; you determine what is right and acceptable and what is not based upon your needs and wants. People blinded by this deception frequently turn to measures other than Christ to determine their so-called self-worth. They seek comfort in money, power, and possessions, but find the comfort is only temporary.

Sometimes people wait too long and never return to the calling upon their heart before they die. Other times, they realize it before time runs out and they come running back to the Lord. The precious mercy of our Savior is that, as long as there is breath in our bodies, it is never too late. See these reassuring words from Psalm 119 –

"Before I was afflicted I went astray, but now I obey your word. You are good, and what you do is good; teach me your decrees."

Psalm 119:67-8

Sleeping Beauty, repent while you can. Repent while your sins are known only to you. Repent before the Lord exposes your sin to others. If you are a child of God, He will spare nothing in His effort to bring you to repentance. When He exposes your sin, it can hurt your family, your job, even your future. The news is full of people who thought they could keep their sin a secret and yet were exposed *in front of the entire world.* The lesson for all of us is clear: deal with yourself in private so God won't do so in public.

Hear my heart for you: God loves *you.* He died *for you.* And He wants to show you the world through His eyes.

Your destiny through Christ is waiting on you. Call out to Him wherever you are and He will forgive and restore you. It is one of the most sacred promises of the Bible and it offers eternal security:

"If we confess our sins, he is faithful and just and will forgive us our sins and purify us from all unrighteousness."

1 John 1:9

The promise is there and ours for the taking. Why would we ever consider not accepting such grace and forgiveness?

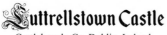

How God Woke Me Up

few years ago, our family company was blindsided by a federal court battle that we never saw coming. We didn't expect it or deserve it, but the battle remained. Without going into all the dreadful details, suffice it to say that the federal government didn't realize they were dealing with what I consider to be the most honest and generous man *ever.*

Still, my husband's character was challenged in every conceivable way. It seems everyone in our small community knew what was going on in matters that are usually considered personal—namely, our financial dealings and taxes. It was a devastating period from start to finish but we knew somehow, the truth would eventually come out. What we didn't know was how long the process would take.

Turns out, nothing moves fast in matters of the federal government. We endured *years* of legal proceedings, delays, turmoil, and uncertainty. It was emotionally draining on our family as well as hard on our business. We had experienced difficult times throughout the years before, but they had all come to pass relatively quickly. In the past, we would endure a season of difficulty for a while and move past it. This season seemed to drag on and on.

Still, throughout the weeks, and eventually years, of this challenge, God put such faith in my heart that I knew beyond a shadow of a doubt that we would be victorious. The promises of Psalm 34 brought me comfort throughout these days:

"The righteous person may have many troubles, but the Lord delivers him from them all;..."

Psalm 34:19

I stood in prayer many times believing and claiming this for our family and our business. It brought me comfort on the darkest of nights when I could almost touch the darkness surrounding our home. At times, it almost felt as if there was an ugly, evil dragon breathing down destruction on us all. My only recourse at these times was to retreat to my prayer room and plead for God to deliver us.

This was my life for almost three years. One night, after I had fallen asleep I had a dream I vividly remembered when

I woke up. In the dream, I saw a woman standing in front of me saying, "God has assigned a warring angel to fight for your deliverance." It gave me courage and hope knowing an angel of God was fighting for me and my family. I know to some people this may sound like a strange memory or even an overactive imagination, but to me, it was confirmation that we could and would get through this court battle and ultimately clear our name and reputation.

My dream reminded me of the vision Daniel had in the Bible when he was told how very precious he was to God. It is a beautiful scene when an angel of the Lord literally speaks hope into Daniel's life. This is what was spoken to Daniel by the angel:

"...'Don't be afraid, Daniel. Since the first day you began to pray for understanding and to humble yourself before your God, your request has been made in heaven. I have come in answer to your prayer. But for twenty-one days the spirit prince of the kingdom of Persia blocked my way. Then Michael, one of the archangels, came to help me, and

I left him there with the spirit prince of the kingdom of Persia.'"

Daniel 10:12-3 (NLT)

In other words, just as there were demonic forces blocking the deliverance of Daniel and a war being waged on his behalf, the Lord delivered him through these injustices, and onto victory.

As the author of Ephesians, Paul wrote this about many of the battles we face throughout our lifetimes:

"For our struggle is not against flesh and blood, but against the rulers, against the authorities, against the powers of this dark world and against the spiritual forces of evil in the heavenly realms."

Ephesians 6:12

Daniel was flesh and blood just like we are. He faced spiritual wickedness just as we do and will continue to face. And most importantly, the Lord delivered him through his battles just as He promises to do for each of us.

Throughout our court battle, these verses filled me with hope. I stood on their promise, believing our family and business would be cleared of any wrongdoing. But it wasn't just these verses that brought me comfort during these tense and trying days. It was many verses that seemed to speak directly to my heart that got me through our ordeal. If I read a verse that seemed appropriate for our situation, I wrote it down and taped it up somewhere in the house. Before long, I had verse upon verse of Scripture all over the house—in my closet, in the bedroom, in the kitchen, garage, and even my car. I wanted to be reminded of God's faithfulness and provision everywhere I went.

As a family, we stood firm on the word of God. We intentionally did not speak negative words to each other or anyone else, but continually spoke of God's word and gave praises that we would be victorious. In doing this, I came to realize that many times in life, it is not what you did wrong, but what you do right to overcome the snares of Satan. The enemy wants nothing more than to destroy your life, your family, and your business. But as believers, we can take courage in knowing that God is fighting for us *every single minute of every single day.*

He wins *every single time.*

The final book of the Bible, Revelation, tells us that Satan will ultimately be defeated. This is how it will be for

the believers who remain in the final days when they face Satan:

> ## "They had power over him and won because of the blood of the Lamb and by telling what He had done for them."
>
> Revelation 12:11 (NLT)

No trouble or problem on earth is too big for the Lord to handle and no trick of the enemy's is too crafty for the Lord to overcome. This is the promise for now *and for eternity*. No matter what you are facing right now or have been through, God is fighting *for you*. With Christ, you are the winner, no matter the outcome, as long as you don't give up.

Everything we go through—good, bad, or mundane—is orchestrated by God. He works every event in your life for your good. Even if He allows you to go through trials and tribulation, you can be assured that it is for a higher purpose and all part of God's plan for your life. No matter the details, the higher purpose in all we experience and endure is for God to get the glory and our hearts to be turned towards Him.

Every day, we are all on a great adventure that should be filled with wonder and surprise at all God has done and continues to do for us. Our great God has a marvelous plan for our lives, and our job is to seek Him and allow ourselves to be used for His glory. When you really take this idea to heart and begin to grasp the intricacies of a God-led life, you can't help but greet each morning with joy and excitement and awe over what beautiful plan He has in store for you today. As daughters of the King, nothing we could ever do can separate us from this unbelievable Christ's love.

And that, Sleeping Beauties, is cause for celebration!

As an update on our legal battles, just as we had believed, we were cleared of all wrongdoings. My husband and our business was completely vindicated and, most importantly, our time of prayer and praising in the months leading up to the trial's conclusion gave us a platform for the Lord. People saw we were facing hard times, yet we relied on the Lord. They saw our business' reputation was being attacked, yet we spoke only positive. And they saw lies were being told about our family yet we found comfort in Christ. In the end, so many people saw the miracle that came through faith.

One of the most positive things that came from my family facing such a devastating time was how it drove me to seek God's word like never before. Night and day, I sought the Lord's insight, looked for words of encouragement, and knelt before the throne. I did this because there was so much at stake. I was petitioning God on behalf of my family and our business—everything that was precious to me. I encourage you, dear sister, whenever you face such a time as we did, give every aspect of your life over to Him. Speak the Word, stand on His promise, and put on the whole armor of God and He will most assuredly defend you and see you through.

The deeper I went with God, the more I was able to see His hand at every turn. The signs and gentle reassurances along the way were truly incredible. I also saw that when I was at my lowest point, God was faithful to share glimpses of His overwhelming love for me. For us, this happened time after time. Just when we felt like we were at rock bottom

emotionally and spiritually, someone would call or send a note of encouragement reminding us that hundreds of people the world over were lifting us up in prayer. It is still so humbling to believe so many interceded on our behalf. We could never thank them all for what meant so very much to our family.

Not long before we became involved in the court battle that tested our tenacity and faith, we had purchased a beautiful 2,000-acre ranch filled with rolling hills and thick, thick forests. It was the perfect retreat for all of us when the pressures of legal troubles became so intense. During these weeks and months, my husband set out to clear much of the ranch of overgrown brush and trees. He enjoyed seeing the fruit of his hard labor and it gave him lots of time alone with God. These escapes did him a world of good in so many ways.

Occasionally our oldest son, Randy, would join him to walk the property and discuss where to place a large lake. As Randy is a civil engineer, his insight was invaluable and his dad especially enjoyed the company and chance to visit with someone he fully trusted.

They eventually decided on what was to be the perfect spot—a beautiful valley that would allow the water to flow into it from all sides. Every time throughout the trial that my husband got the chance, he would drive the two hours to the ranch and hop aboard the huge bulldozer we had parked out there and work for hours upon hours digging deeper and deeper for the new lake. From the outside, it looked like he was putting in a full day's work of hard labor, but to him, it became his prayer time. The fruit from these digging sessions soon became obvious—his faith grew deeper and deeper, just as the lake did. When he came to fully accept that the Lord was in total control of our situation *no matter what,* he knew what people meant when they spoke of 'the peace that passes understanding.'

Because this whole lake-digging adventure was new to all of us, I asked how long it would take for it to be full. As the lake covered acres and acres of land, my husband said it would take at least a year, but probably closer to a year and a half or more.

And then we experienced what we believe to be a miracle.

It began to rain and rain and rain. It went on for so many days, I thought this must have been what it was like in the days of Noah when there seemed to be no end to the rains. And the lake…the lake that was predicted to take at least a year to fill…it was completely full in less than a month! It rained so fast and so hard, my husband barely had time to get the bulldozer out of the hole before it was underwater. Everyone in our family felt like it was God assuring us and telling us, "I have heard your prayer."

We named the lake 'Memorial Lake' and I even had a rock engraved with a scripture that was particularly meaningful to us. It is found in Acts:

"...your prayers and gifts to the poor have come up as a memorial offering to God."

Acts 10:4

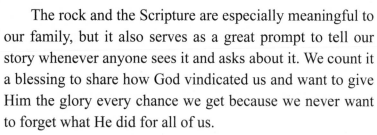

The rock and the Scripture are especially meaningful to our family, but it also serves as a great prompt to tell our story whenever anyone sees it and asks about it. We count it a blessing to share how God vindicated us and want to give Him the glory every chance we get because we never want to forget what He did for all of us.

My wake-up call was a treacherous journey; I wouldn't wish it upon anyone. But now that we're on the other side of the turmoil I can see that my faith grew and grew during this time. I began to hunger for the Bible and worked to listen to His voice like never before. I was reminded time after time that I had encountered a loving God that still had a purpose for my life.

Just as it was for me, when you are fully awake, you begin to see things more clearly and believe there is a destiny for your life. I hope with all my heart that you don't experience the darkest days I did, but that you wake up *now* to the call of God upon your life. Ask Him to awaken you to the beauty and majesty of His Kingdom. There are people— more than you could begin to grasp—that are waiting on *you* to offer them the hope of Christ. You never know who is looking at you as the example of a woman who has woken to the call of Christ on her life.

Always remember, Sleeping Beauty, that when you completely trust God, you can rest in the promise that everything will work out for your good.

Castle Durrow

Durrow, Co. Laois, Ireland

8

HIS PURPOSE FOR SLEEPING BEAUTIES

here is no one like you on the planet. *No one.* When God made you, he created you to have a purpose that is unique just to you. Though others may travel similar paths, have common interests or strengths or personality traits, your God-designed purpose is for you alone.

The outside trappings of life, such as if you are single or married, rich or poor, chic or simple, don't matter in terms of fulfilling your destiny. What does matter is that, to completely and fully live out your purpose, you must surrender your life to God and allow Him to cover you with His supernatural covering of grace. Psalm 91 is one of my favorite passages

in the entire Bible because of the reassurance we are given as believers. It promises us safety and protection and comfort when we claim the 'Most High' as our protector.

This is a partial version of the Scripture:

"Whoever dwells in the shelter of the Most High will rest in the shadow of the Almighty. I will say of the Lord, 'He is my refuge and my fortress, my God, in whom I trust.' Surely, He will save you from the fowler's snare and from the deadly pestilence. He will cover you with his feathers, and under His wings you will find refuge; His faithfulness will be your shield and rampart. You will not fear the terror of night, nor the arrow that flies by day,"

Psalm 91:1-5

"If you say, 'The Lord is my refuge,' and you make the Most High your dwelling, no harm will overtake you, no disaster will come near your tent. For he will command his angels concerning you To guard you in all your ways;..."

Psalm 91:9-11

"... 'Because he loves me,' says the Lord, 'I will rescue him; I will protect him, for he acknowledges My name. He will call on me and I will answer him; I will be with him in trouble, I will deliver him and honor him With long life I will satisfy him and show him My salvation.'"

Psalm 91:14-16

There are so many Sleeping Beauties who live in such incredible fear. They fear things real and things imagined; things they think they can control and things they know they can't, and things of tremendous concern and things of little consequence. They fear people they know and even those they don't; they fear what has happened in the past and what might happen in the future; and they fear so much and so many, there isn't room for both God and all their fears.

Fear rules their life.

But as a daughter of the living God—the King of Kings—none of us should live surrounded by fear. He has equipped each of us with many, many gifts that only we can fully realize and utilize when we listen to His voice.

When you are fully awake and walking in step with the Lord, you can understand the magnitude of this precious, precious gift—*your* uniquely fashioned, divinely-directed life. Again, no matter the trappings of your life, past or present, you are God's by design. It doesn't matter who your parents are (or were), where you were raised, how big your house is or how much you have in the bank. What matters is that you are blessedly and most assuredly *HIS,* and God has a purpose for you to fulfill.

I know of many women who didn't have what most

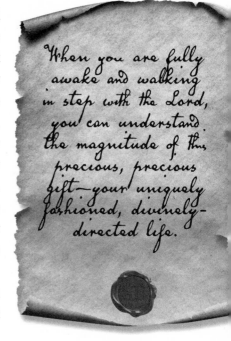

When you are fully awake and walking in step with the Lord, you can understand the magnitude of this precious, precious gift—your uniquely fashioned, divinely-directed life.

would consider a good childhood. Their days were not carefree and full of play and imagination; many of them dealt with abuse and neglect and were too young to do anything about it. The good news is that doesn't have to define who they are *now* and where they go from here. It's the same for you. No matter your history, you get to choose *from this moment on* to have a more abundant life when you make the decision to follow Christ.

As an example from the Bible, Queen Esther began her life as an orphan. She had an unusual childhood because she was raised by her uncle. Because of this, she probably had a much different outlook than many little girls her age because she saw many things from her only caregiver's perspective—a man's outlook. This helped her to be unique in lots of beneficial ways because she came to understand how a man would look at and think about different situations. In the end, God used her untraditional upbringing to help her save her people.

Today, God is raising up women to a new level of authority and a new place to lead from. The modern-day Esther is full of purpose and passion for what she believes God has called her to accomplish. She has the potential to capture the attention of her city, her country, maybe even the world. A woman that has awakened to her purpose will walk with her head held high because she is following God's lead for her life. She knows she is representing the King of Kings and that allows her to be humble yet speak and act with kingdom authority.

This was certainly the case for Esther, though it took a bit of persuading by Mordecai for her to move forward. In Esther, Chapter 4, Mordecai is appealing to Esther for her to

accept the call upon her life to save not only herself, but her people as well. This is what he says to her:

> # "'Do not think that because you are in the king's house you alone of all the Jews will escape. For if you remain silent at this time, relief and deliverance for the Jews will arise from another place, but you and your father's family will perish. And who knows but that you have come to your royal position for such a time as this?'"

Esther 4:13-14

He makes a pretty compelling argument, doesn't he? He's telling her that if she doesn't speak up and act on her people's behalf, she's a goner. And so is her family. And somebody else will lead her people to safety while she remains and perishes. I can't help but think if I were in Esther's position back then and someone had said this to me, I wouldn't have wanted anybody else speaking for me or taking my place when the Lord had put it upon my heart to do so.

Even when the circumstances are frightening or seem overwhelming, we have to remember Divine Providence has placed us where we are and it will see us through. And even if no one else understands, our privilege as believers is to consider our purpose and work to fulfill it. Esther realized the dangers she faced were small compared to losing her people and her soul. She knew she had to fulfill her purpose and find courage in her faith to take her request before the King in order to save the Jews. It was not a time to be silent and allow others to suffer, including herself and her family.

For far too long women have been silent and allowed unrighteous people to speak for us. The time has come for us to be brave and to speak the truth as we know it with boldness. We have the opportunity to step up and speak for our families, our neighborhoods, and our country. There is so much for us to step forward and save!

Now is the time for women of all ages to answer this call. Energetic, enthusiastic young mamas as well as older, more experienced women are needed to step up to this call of purpose. In my travels throughout the world, I have seen the beauty of older women coming alongside of younger women teaching them the ways of

God. They are sharing the maturity and insight of many years of growing their faith with women who are just now coming into their own. It gives me so much hope to see these different generations walking hand-in-hand. Nothing could be more powerful than the shared insight and energy of these women partnering for Christ. I believe they will be able to command the authority the Kingdom deserves and spark a new awakening for future generations.

If you don't yet have the benefit of another woman who can guide and direct you in the ways of God, I would challenge you to find one. Or maybe even a few. One may be well-versed in Old Testament teachings and another know more about the New Testament. Also, get into a Bible study and become intentional about learning God's word and the history of his people. You'll learn from women of the Bible as well as your teachers and those learning alongside of you. I think you'll soon realize how incredibly capable women have been and continue to be.

We know how to get things done, how to love on and encourage others, and how to serve. We can cut through the clutter and see the real issue at hand, oftentimes bringing answers to complicated issues. And we can multitask—we can multitask like no other creature on earth!

I remember when I was a young mom with two small children and a husband starting a new company. I felt like I had no real value. I spent every day taking care of my babies, cooking, cleaning, and trying to be a good wife to my husband. There were days I wanted to cry myself to sleep because I felt as if I had no real purpose.

This was in a stark contrast to my life before kids and marriage. Just a few years earlier, I had been an executive assistant to a then-famous celebrity and was also a professional singer. I worked my regular job during the week and on the weekends, would fly in private jets to singing engagements. The glamour of it all—the beautiful, colorful clothes, the open-ended expense account, the audiences—all were thrilling—at least in the beginning.

I learned so many things then that would later help in building our company and entertaining. At the time, however, I didn't have a clue what God was trying to teach me and how He was equipping me for the days ahead. I remember one day while I was in Miami, I fell on my knees and said a prayer that sounded something like this:

"I don't feel like this is where I am supposed to be. I know I have a purpose, but I need a word from you, God. Please show me what to do and give me the desires of my heart. I don't even know what they are, but please God, if you're listening, please tell me."

I also began to regularly pray Psalm 37:4:

"Be happy in the Lord. And He will give you the desires of your heart."

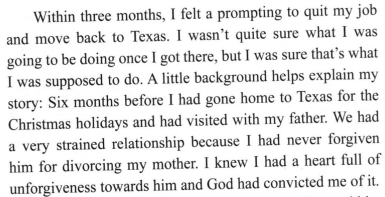

Within three months, I felt a prompting to quit my job and move back to Texas. I wasn't quite sure what I was going to be doing once I got there, but I was sure that's what I was supposed to do. A little background helps explain my story: Six months before I had gone home to Texas for the Christmas holidays and had visited with my father. We had a very strained relationship because I had never forgiven him for divorcing my mother. I knew I had a heart full of unforgiveness towards him and God had convicted me of it.

I told my dad I was sorry for my anger and begged him for his forgiveness. What I hadn't expected was that *he* began to weep. He told me how sorry he was, that the whole thing had been his fault, and then he asked for *my* forgiveness. It was one of the most healing conversations I've ever had. On top of that, he ultimately introduced me to the man who would become my husband!

After the holidays, I returned to my job in Florida and my dad started calling me every week telling me I *just had to meet* this young man who went to his church. Although I appreciated him thinking of me, in my mind I was thinking, "Are you kidding me? All your friends spend most of their time in the woods hunting and fishing. I am a city girl!"

But dad and God had other ideas.

When I felt the call to return to Texas six months later, I did, in fact, meet the man my dad had been telling me about for so long. Turns out, dad was right. He was the man of my dreams and we were married three months later.

The moral of this story for me and for you, too, is to forgive and forget. Whoever and whatever has hurt you or broken you, give it to God and put it under the blood of Jesus. Give it to Him and quit carrying the burden of anger and resentment and pain. If you don't move past it and allow God to carry it for you, you might just end up missing your destiny.

But back to my endless days of diapers and housework. Don't get me wrong—I was still very thankful for my precious husband and kids and our home, but it was a far departure from the glitz and glam I had been a part of just a year or two before. I would see some of the people I used to work with and perform with on television or in the fashion magazines and I began to feel more than just a bit sorry for myself. Gone were the jets and exciting lifestyle; we didn't even have enough extra money for me to buy some new and more fashionable clothes at the time.

I missed all the extras—the fancy things of my previous life—but mostly I just felt like I didn't have a real purpose. All I could see ahead of me were more diapers, more dinners to be cooked, and more laundry to fold. I couldn't see the big picture of what my life was becoming. Looking back, now I know it was a lie from the deepest, darkest pit of hell, straight from the mouth of Satan. *Now I know,* now that I have the precious gift of hindsight, that there is nothing more valuable than a mother loving and caring for her children and building a godly home. *Nothing.*

Sometimes, I've learned, the voice of deception can be so loud that it drowns out the voice of God. It can be hard to hear God through all the clutter the world throws our way... hard, but *not impossible.* And it's most certainly worth the effort.

One day I cried out to God and I heard a voice in my spirit tell me, "Judy, if you will be honorable and faithful to your husband, and if you will raise these boys and teach them

to walk in my ways, I promise I will bless you so much and in so many ways that you will never have need of anything for the rest of your life."

From that moment on, I began to praise God, thanking Him for my husband and children. His Word became alive in me as I learned to pray scriptures over my family and our growing business. These verses brought special comfort to me:

"The Lord announces the word, and the women who proclaim it are a might throng; 'Kings and armies flee in haste; the women at home divide the plunder.'"

Psalm 68:11-12

This scripture stood out to me because I realized I could fight the warfare of the enemy *wherever I was, whatever I was doing*. This meant, that in the middle of a toddler meltdown or picking up toys for the hundredth time that day, I could stand on the Word of God and declare a blessing over our home and our business. There was no end to where I could fight the enemy and call on the name of God!

So many women today need to realize this and begin fighting *now*. Just because you can't see what is ahead of you, don't allow the enemy to distract you from your purpose. We all go through seasons of our lives and every season serves its own distinct purpose. If God has called you *now* for a season of raising children, embrace it and don't be ashamed to do so. If God has called you to work in a career outside the home, ask Him to direct the course of your career for His glory. Whatever path you pursue, your life will become a beautiful tapestry when you follow the path chosen distinctly for you.

Not far from our ranch is a beautiful little country church. Every Thanksgiving, they host a community fair and many of the women bring beautiful blankets and quilts they have sewn over the past year. They come in all shapes and sizes, colors, and designs. Every time I see all these bits and pieces of different fabrics woven together, it reminds me of my life—bits and pieces from different seasons that have brought me where I am today. Every experience, every memory, and every relationship I have with my husband, my children, and my friends are all woven together to create this beautiful life of mine. Not every experience has been enjoyable at the time, but the fruit that has come from going through it has always been a beautiful thing.

I believe in the days to come, God is going to use women not only in their home lives, but also in the business and financial world. I think women, especially godly women, will be called upon to answer some of the world's most

Whatever path you pursue, your life will become a beautiful tapestry when you follow the path chosen distinctly for you.

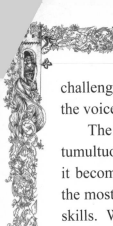

challenging questions. Because of this, Satan wants to quiet the voice of these would-be Sleeping Beauties.

The enemy knows women can bring peace and calm to tumultuous situations. We can diffuse a disagreement before it becomes explosive. And we can encourage others to do the most good for the most people because of our relational skills. Wherever your strengths lie, use them and your identity in Christ to impact the world for Him. Always remember that you are a daughter of the King, dressed in royal robes, and adorned with a crown of righteousness. Yours is a holy calling.

Don't allow sleepless nights to impact your reach. No more! You are called for such a time as this. You have a purpose to fulfill, beautiful daughter of Zion. Don't allow the expectations of the world define you; ask God to define and refine you and to speak over your life. Hear the encouragements of from the Book of Zephaniah:

> "'The Lord your God is with you, the Mighty Warrior who saves. He will take great delight in you; in his love he will no longer rebuke you, but will rejoice over you with singing.'"

Zephaniah 3:17

How wonderful is that? The Lord, *our God,* will rejoice over us! Even if you didn't grow up with a kind and loving father, you now can have a heavenly Father who surrounds you with His never-ending love. He created *the entire universe* to take delight in you. He will sing over you at all times and give you peace in the midst of life's harshest storms. In times of rebellion and hurt, He commands that we repent; in moments of brokenness and despair, He bathes us in His grace.

He wants our whole being—heart, mind, body, and soul. So today, humble yourself before Him and ask for these things: passion, discernment, power, provision, blessing, and favor. In doing so, you become free from the snares of the enemy. Your chains are broken and you are free to pursue your purpose and vision.

It's your day. Don't let *anyone* stop you from fulfilling the destiny God has designed for you.

Lough Eske Castle

Lough Eske, Co. Donegal, Ireland

9

SLEEPING BEAUTIES FROM AROUND THE WORLD

hen God gave me the mandate to help 'wake the sleeping beauties,' I had no idea this calling would take me around the world—literally! I stepped out in faith, not knowing how this vision would manifest itself, and believe me, the adventures of following Christ's call upon your heart and your life are never boring!

One of the most reassuring ways the Lord has spoken to me throughout this journey is by allowing me to see His hand in every detail along the way and preparing me well in advance for each new phase. For example, I have been teaching a Bible study for over 10 years now at our

second ranch, Shenandoah Ranch. This is our 'city ranch' because it is much closer to town and where we live most of the time. Our other piece of land is much further away and truly considered 'in the country.' We are beyond blessed to have both parcels of land and consider it a fulfillment of Deuteronomy 28:1-3 to be so tremendously blessed. This is what it says:

> "**If you fully obey the Lord your God and carefully follow all his commands I give you today, the Lord your God will set you high above all the nations on earth. All these blessings will come on you and accompany you if you obey the Lord your God: You will be blessed in the city and blessed in the country.**"

Deuteronomy 28:1-3

Please know we don't consider ourselves to be 'fully obedient' even a good amount of the time. We let our human nature get the better of us and have its way with us all too many times. We do, however, do the best we can and are always intentionally working towards getting better in matters of obedience. It is a day-by-day challenge, but a worthy one!

Back to the ranch—the very name of our home, Shenandoah Ranch, means 'great singers.' And that couldn't be more perfect! Every Tuesday night, dozens and dozens of women gather together here to worship and study the Bible with one another. What I didn't realize, however, is that during all these years of studying and teaching, the Lord was preparing me—my heart, my soul, and my mind—all of me! for the adventure He had in mind for me down the road.

I know from experience that I'm not alone in regard to the Lord preparing me so well in advance before revealing my actual calling. Many women I know can look back and see how experiences and lessons from their past were paving the way for the grander calling God had for them. We just didn't know it at the time. That's one of the reasons why I think it's so important to remember that, sometimes, you have to wait for the season to which you have been called.

Divine callings *cannot* be rushed.

When the time is right, God will allow any- and everything you need to fall into place. In the meantime, study His word, dream grand dreams, prepare the best way you know how, and pray to be ready whenever He calls you to your destiny. Years ago, all I knew was that I was called to teach a weekly Bible study; I had no idea my faithfulness to this call would lead to a much bigger platform. But it did and continues to do so *in the most wonderfully fulfilling ways!*

And I rejoice every day for this calling upon my life.

As I mentioned in an earlier chapter, I can trace my calling to waken the sleeping beauties of this world back to the day I was on my way to a luncheon celebrating missions. I consider this my 'Esther Call,' because I knew, at that exact moment, that I was being called upon by God to help others.

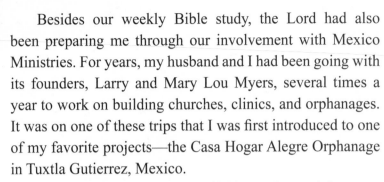

Besides our weekly Bible study, the Lord had also been preparing me through our involvement with Mexico Ministries. For years, my husband and I had been going with its founders, Larry and Mary Lou Myers, several times a year to work on building churches, clinics, and orphanages. It was on one of these trips that I was first introduced to one of my favorite projects—the Casa Hogar Alegre Orphanage in Tuxtla Gutierrez, Mexico.

Since first becoming a part of this precious ministry, we have returned most Christmases with a team from Texas to love on and minister to these kids. We take as many as 80-100 children to buy clothes, underwear, socks, shoes—just the basics that so many of us take for granted. We always end our shopping sprees with a stop by McDonald's. We order burgers and fries by the dozens and then my husband always turns to the manager and says, "Get the ice cream cones ready! We only need 100!" The look on these sweet children's faces afterwards makes all the time and effort worth every second.

Besides the children at the orphanage, we also try to regularly visit the children way up the mountainside that are part of the indigenous Chiapas people. We come with bags and bags of candy and boxes upon boxes of shoes. The children can't believe their good fortune when they receive these small treats, but we're truly the ones who receive the greater blessing as part of this missions team.

The orphanage and the children in the nearby villages have impacted our lives so much that we have remained active and engaged with them for many years. They have touched our hearts forever with their gratitude over such simple gifts. Through the years, it has been such a tremendous joy to see the children grow in their schooling as well as their understanding of deep Biblical truths.

So many great, great people have partnered with us throughout the years as we have worked to minister to these little ones. Many, many people provide money and resources to make these trips happen, but we are the fortunate ones allowed to make the trips and see the sweet, sweet faces of these children living without running water, a stable shelter, or even shoes for their tiny feet. It is a joy beyond belief to wipe the mud and dirt from their feet and replace it with a brand, new pair of shoes. Their joy is off-the-charts and our crew…well, we do our best to see through the tears in our eyes.

All these years of working alongside my husband with Mexico Ministries put within my heart a great love for international ministry. The more involved I became, the more I realized that there are so unbelievably many needs throughout the world, it's overwhelming. Do you help these people or those? Do you take supplies to this country or that one? Do you focus on just children or everyone in the village? It's enough to make your head spin! In my heart, I wanted to meet each new need more than the last, but knew I couldn't. So, I did the next best thing: *I did what I could to help those I could.*

So, back to the day of the luncheon—it was sponsored by Global Advance and the new ministry opportunities they were launching. The two that stood out to me were the Esther Initiative and the Marketplace Missions. Even though we had supported the team at Global Advance for years, it wasn't until that day that I began to see the 'big picture' of what they were working towards and who they were serving.

Jonathan Shibley, president of the organization, opened the luncheon with a vision for a new ministry that would focus primarily on women around the world. I was immediately intrigued and knew it was God stirring my heart to learn more. They had been pursuing this ministry in more than 100 countries for over 27 years, but they wanted to reach more women in more ways and in more countries.

I knew in my heart that this was my season.

This was my calling.

And so, with my husband's blessing, I began a journey around the world to answer the call upon my heart. The first call--to help women—seemed like a natural for me, so I knew the Esther Initiative would be a terrific fit; and the second, Marketplace Missions was an opportunity for me to put to use all my unique perspective as a woman experienced in commercial construction. All my years as a wife, mom, and businesswoman were bearing fruit as I prepared for this next, exciting chapter in my life.

Looking back, I can see, in one day, how dramatically my life changed *for the better.* A door opened to opportunities that I had literally been preparing for my entire life.

From there, the divine appointments around the world quickly began to unfold. I began to meet men and women who would significantly change my life from that point forward. God allowed me to hear stories from all across the world about how lives were being changed through our ministries. It was one blessing after another; each story more amazing than the one before it.

I could talk for weeks—*really!*—about the hundreds of stories I've heard since that exciting day, but several stand out above all the rest. The first one is about Rosa. She is a mother of five who lives high in the mountains of Chiapas, Mexico, and she loves the Lord with all her heart. Even though she has lived in extreme poverty her whole life, she faithfully served God and never gave up on her dream to someday provide for her family.

Every day she would work to weave clothing from sheared sheep or walk to gather sticks for firewood to sell for money. Rosa's roots run deep in this region; her people are descendants from the ancient Mayans some 1,500+ years ago. She became a Christ-follower many years ago at a mountainside revival when God woke her to His calling upon her life. At the time, Rosa and her children lived in a hut with no running water and a dirt floor, but God heard the call of her heart to provide for her family.

Today, you might not even recognize Rosa from the woman she used to be. Though she still dresses in her native, handwoven traditional dress, now she is considered something akin to royalty among her people. Now she and her children live in a three-story concrete home—*complete with running water!* From her third floor patio you can look out and see the Sierra Madre Mountains stretching out before you. You can also see dozens and dozens of tiny huts, much like the one Rosa used to live in, as a reminder of where she used to be.

When I last visited her home, I was overcome with a single thought: God loves Rosa. He heard the cry of her heart and He blessed her. It was such a gentle reminder that the blessing of God can be anywhere and to anyone. It doesn't matter where you live, how you live, the color of your skin, or who you are—the blessing of God is a covenant promise for all of us who believe.

Since first getting to know Rosa, her children have mostly grown up, but all of them are active in ministry. Several of them serve at the clinic next door that treats hundreds of people each year—all free of charge thanks to Mexico Ministries. Her son is the local pastor and helped to build the most majestic church in the area that rises high above the city.

Each year, over 5,000 indigenous people come to the church for a conference. And each year, you'll find Rosa, her husband, three daughters, and two sons serving these thousands of people. Rosa is an exceptional example of a Sleeping Beauty who was awakened to the call of God upon her heart. She held fast to the promise that God would provide and hear her prayers and she is changed woman because of it. But not only is she changed, the course of her entire family's life is changed, too. Generations will be blessed because of Rosa's faithfulness and her obedience to the call upon her life—all of this from a hut with no water and no floor.

Every year we see one another, she gives me the gift of a handwoven blouse. We pray together and *always* cry when it comes time for our team to leave. And every year, as our van pulls away, I am reminded that I have been blessed to be in the presence of a woman considered to be a royal queen in her own native land.

Elizabeth Castelazo Noguera is a Sleeping Beauty that you will never forget once you've heard her story. She started an orphanage for the abused, abandoned, and neglected children of Tuxtla Gutierrez, Mexico. This is the same orphanage we visit each year at Christmastime. Elizabeth didn't set out to run an orphanage; it just happened as a result of her obedience to God. One by one, she began taking in children into her teeny, tiny house. She barely had money to provide, but she knew God had put a desire in her heart to help these children and so she did.

Today, Elizabeth provides food, shelter, clothes, and education for over 100 boys and girls in her town. Many of the children brought to her have been found living on the streets or abandoned by their families. It is impossible to hold one of these children on your lap, see their smile, and hear their laughter without being moved by compassion to want to help them. Throughout the years, watching these children that were once abandoned children become fine young men and women is one of the joys of my life.

Their stories would have been drastically different had it not been for Elizabeth. She could have said 'no' to the call, but she was confident that somehow, God would provide for each child she brought in. And He did…and then some.

Every time we visit with 'Mama Elizabeth,' she has a new set of plans or drawings for a building she wants to build for the children God woke her up to serve. She has grand visions because she was awakened by God. And because she knows that nothing is impossible when you answer His call.

Halfway across the world, I was blessed to meet another Sleeping Beauty and discover the most unique job title I've ever heard of: a *paid* intercessor of prayer. That's right—I met a woman who is *paid to pray*. I learned of her when I was visiting a tool company in Germany that had been in business for over a hundred years. The company has done a very good job of keeping up with the times as they were modernized and streamlined throughout the factory, but they were also obviously very committed to the power of prayer.

The company has beautiful offices, a large warehouse, and lots of employees. They are also committed to making a difference in the lives of their employees and well beyond their corporate doors. After lunch with company leaders one day, I learned they truly 'practice what they preach' by giving 10% of everything they make to help others in their community. That's an impressive track record for anyone or any company and then…then, I met the woman who was *the paid prayer intercessor.*

Curious, I asked the owner of the company how they came to establish such a unique position for their company. He explained that, when they bought the company, it was failing, but that God had put it upon his heart he needed someone on-staff committed to praying for the business full-time. *A full-time prayer!* And now, he explained, the business is sustained by her prayers.

I had to know more about this woman. She told me how God had put in her heart a passion to pray. She wasn't skilled in anything the company made or sold, but she was skilled in prayer. She was obedient to her calling and her company was obedient to its calling.

If you have been called to intercede on behalf of others as a prayer warrior--on behalf of your family, your business, your world--rest assured, Sleeping Beauty, you have received a noble calling.

Let this be encouragement to you, if ever you doubt you can make a difference in people's lives. If you have been called to intercede on behalf of others as a prayer warrior--on behalf of your family, your business, your world--rest assured, Sleeping Beauty, you have received a noble calling. You can and will make a difference with your prayers!

I've had the blessing of serving with several other ministries as I've traveled throughout the world. One of them, Latin Equip, brought me to Lima, Peru, where I experienced God's presence and holiness in the most extraordinary way. I had met the mission's founders, Steve and Shelly Hopkins, at the Lima airport, and our crew decided to have lunch there before heading out.

The backstory here is this: our group had passed through Lima several days earlier on our way to presenting a conference in another city *and* we had had lunch at this same restaurant before we boarded our out-bound plane. We even had the same waitress both times. Still, it was a surprise when she came to take our orders this second time and asked, "Do you want to order the same thing you did a few days ago?"

We were all stunned. Surely, she had waited on dozens, if not hundreds, of people since first serving us lunch four days earlier. How could she possibly remember us *and our order* out of all the people she had served since then? I started talking to her through our translator and asked how she so easily remembered us. She told us it was easy—we were happy and smiling.

I shared with her that we were that way because we were Christians and that we had been called 'to wake up the sleeping beauties' of the world to their calling within Christ. We told her how much God loved her and asked her if she wanted to commit her life to Christ *then and there.* She immediately began to cry and said, "Yes! Yes!"

She went on to explain that her life up to that point had been a complete mess and that she wanted to give up on everything. She said she felt hopeless, with no future, and no way out. We assured her that she was anything but hopeless because today was her day! And so, right there in the middle of the airport restaurant, with lots of people waiting for their food, we prayed for her to receive Christ into her heart. She knew her other tables needed servicing, but she couldn't stop crying and praising God. All of us were overcome with joy for her.

While we were celebrating her decision, another waitress came over and told us, "I have been praying for her for over a year to accept Christ. Thank you for taking the time to share with her today." Right there—in the middle of the airport—Christ showed up and we had a revival. A woman's heart was changed and we were blessed to play a small part in it.

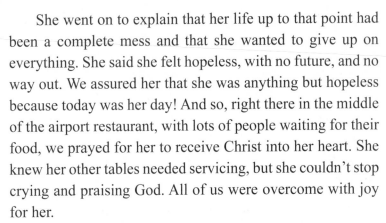

This is just how God works—He orchestrates the unexpected, the improbable, the seemingly impossible just to reach the lonely and the lost.

This sweet and surprising encounter with our waitress helped me to remember that we never know where or when God will show up. Even though we came to Peru to put on conferences for hundreds of women, this might have been the most important stop of the whole trip. This is just how God works—He orchestrates the unexpected, the improbable, the seemingly impossible just to reach the lonely and the lost. Whatever the circumstances or wherever the setting, I am constantly reminded that God gave His life for one beautiful soul after another.

I have so many stories of God's presence and power from around the world, I could go on and on, but I'll leave you with one last story that I hope builds your faith as much as it has mine. It happened only a few years ago in the Dominican Republic when I was speaking at a women's conference there. Our team was staying at the home of a very wealthy man from Venezuela. There was a staff of seven to bring us anything we could imagine. It was unbelievably luxurious!

The pastor of the local church had become friends with this man who, in turn, would always allow conference speakers to stay in his extraordinary home. Ironically, my husband called later in the day from his mission trip *on the other side of the world!* While he was backpacking in Mongolia, sleeping in a ger (a portable, round tent) in 27-degree weather, I told him of the palace we were staying in, complete with swimming pool and sunny, 82-degree weather. When he told me my accommodations didn't sound much like those usually available on mission trips, we both laughed and I told him, "I am a daughter of the King! And He likes to surprise me!"

On this particular day, I also had the privilege of meeting two women, Yovanka and Tania. Yovanka was the interior designer for the estate and had come to begin the redecorating process. I told her about our conference and she said, "So you are a Christian? I am, too!" This simple bond was the beginning of a precious friendship that continues today.

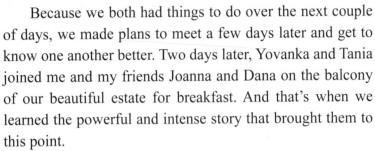

Because we both had things to do over the next couple of days, we made plans to meet a few days later and get to know one another better. Two days later, Yovanka and Tania joined me and my friends Joanna and Dana on the balcony of our beautiful estate for breakfast. And that's when we learned the powerful and intense story that brought them to this point.

They had both studied in Paris and traveled the world in earlier years. They had great wealth and success, but had also experienced much sorrow until they came to know Christ. First, Yovanka shared how she had been married to a very wealthy man and had had a child. When she became pregnant a second time, she also learned her best friend had been having an adulterous relationship with her husband and was pregnant by him, too.

From there, she said, her life began to spiral out of control. She was devastated by this discovery and spent every day afterward locked in her room, either crying uncontrollably or staring at the walls. When she finally felt able to move forward, she said to herself, "I am going to find the richest man in the Dominican Republic. I don't care if he's handsome or ugly. I just want someone who will give me all the money I can possibly spend." In the meantime, she also studied to become a Buddhist as part of her transformational journey.

Before too long, she found herself in a relationship with one of the richest men on the island. But, she was still miserable. Then she remembered—her mother had been through a similar experience with the men in her life and she, too, had gone into deep depression afterwards. She realized she was under a generational curse, but she didn't understand exactly what that meant or know how to break free.

Even though she had all the money she could ever need, she was still lacking in purpose—something that mattered. A friend had told her about an orphanage nearby that was looking for volunteers and she began volunteering there within a few weeks. One of the little girls at the orphanage sang quite well and even made a recording for Yovanka. She would take it home and listen to it over and over and hear this sweet, young voice singing about a Savior. She said she would cry as she listened. But they weren't sad tears; they were *happy tears—tears that surrounded her with peace.*

Her story goes on to tell that a famous Latin singer, Juan Luis Guerra, was coming to the Dominican Republic and wanted to hear the young girl's recording and possibly help the orphanage in some way. A mutual acquaintance arranged for Yovanka to meet Guerra, but Yovanka was very resistant. Still so depressed by the betrayal of her husband and the life she was now living, Yovanka had grown used to spending much of her time crying and was in no frame of mind to meet the singer even if it was for the orphanage's benefit.

She finally decided to go to the arranged meeting and, while waiting for the singer, she met the director of the orphanage who was also there to meet with the singer. While waiting, he noticed her swollen eyes and asked if she was okay. She told him a little about her story before he was called into his meeting with Guerra.

A few minutes later, both the director and Guerra walked out of their meeting and laid their hands on her head and began to pray for her. And then things turned supernatural: Juan began singing over her. A world-famous singer, in this beautiful villa, praying and singing over her! Within minutes,

Yovanka says a supernatural presence of peace came over her as she began to cry in surrender to God.

Immediately, she felt as if everything about her was changing as the chains of darkness and fear were broken and she was finally free. She knew, then and there, that she didn't need material possessions or a man to give her comfort and peace; she needed a savior. She severed her relationship with the man she had been seeing and returned home to rid herself of every Buddhist idol she had. She was changed forever in an instant.

Yovanka's story is not over. Every time I talk to her, I am amazed at how God delivered her from such extreme darkness and sadness. God has met her every step of her journey to be closer to her. Her design business has flourished, her personal life is much better, and most importantly, she walks each day alongside her Savior. Not long ago I had dinner with Yovanka and Tania and they were both incredible testimonies of redemption. Tania and her husband live in a tropical paradise in Casa de Campo, full of waterfalls and beautiful palm trees.

On this particular night, we had dinner out on the patio and it was a night I will never forget. Yes, it was one of the most beautiful villas I have ever seen, but the most meaningful memory of the night was how both women gave glory and praise to God for 'waking them up!'

These two women are making an impact on the Dominican Republic by mentoring and teaching other women about the love of God. They understand that once they were lost in sin and darkness, but when they met their Savior, everything changed. In their own way, they are waking up their kingdom. I am proud to call her one of my dearest friends on the planet.

Sleeping Beauty, I want so much for you to be encouraged by these stories of radically changed women. These women are no different than you are in so many ways. They've faced difficult days and wonderful days; they've known despair and delight, and they've all come to the same conclusion: we all need Jesus. They know *what you can know*: it doesn't matter where you were born, your education level, your status in life or the number in your bank account—we all need a savior. We all need to know that we have the Prince of Peace and the King of Kings always ready, willing, and more than able to wake us from our slumber and lead us to our destiny.

Your past is no challenge for the glory of your future when you awaken to the Savior's call upon your life.

Lough Rynn Castle

Mohill, Co. Leitrim, Ireland

10

GOD HAS A MASTER PLAN FOR SLEEPING BEAUTIES

y husband had just recently had surgery and was spending a couple of days recuperating in the hospital. I was there most of the time to keep him company and make sure he had everything he needed and wanted. One day I noticed just outside his hospital window there was a large, new construction project going up. Our windows were large, floor-to-ceiling panes so we had an incredible, bird's-eye view of the six-story building going up beside us.

Since most of our adult life has been involved in the construction business, I had particular interest in watching how things were done, what order they were done in, and how the workers went about their jobs and handled all the machinery. On this particular day, there were hundreds of workers on the job and they all seemed to be doing something different. Some were on different levels of the building putting up structural steel, nailing sheetrock to the supports, or installing electrical lines. Others were on the ground, driving tractors, forklifts, and all sorts of other equipment that's necessary for commercial construction. There was even a tower crane that could lift heavy loads of materials off the ground and raise them to the sixth floor. It was fascinating to watch everyone going about their particular job, yet each ultimately contributing to the building's completion.

The tower crane reached at least 100 feet above ground and the area around it looked like a sea of workers in bright yellow safety vests and hard hats. Everyone knew what they were supposed to be doing to keep things running smoothly and did so. Their day began at 6:30 a.m. and ended at 3:30 and appeared to operate like well-oiled machinery with everything in sync. It was inspiring to watch their commitment to their job, their attention to detail, and the precision with which they carried out their jobs.

As I watched this highly choreographed process of modern construction, I felt in my heart that God was speaking to me. I stopped to consider that this one project—this one six-story building—consisted of hundreds of pages of plans. And thousands of feet of structural steel. And miles upon miles of electrical wiring. And even though there is a master plan, with all of these specifics, most of the workers will never see the vision for the completed project. All they'll see is their task at hand; what they are responsible for; what they need to know *here and now*, not sometime in the future.

There will be page after page of structural engineering plans and drawings, civil engineering estimates, detailed electrical and mechanical plans and contingencies, and much more, but the bottom line is this: Other than the architect, the general contractor, and the project foreman, few others will ever see the full set of drawings for this building. But that day as I was looking at the entire project from our third-floor window, I thought,

"This is how God sees it all because He can see the masterplan."

Our lives are how it was with this construction site: Just as each of these construction workers didn't know the details of what every other worker was doing, we don't know what is going on in other people's lives and homes. But there is a masterplan and God is the original architect. He holds all the plans and it doesn't matter that we see it or what we understand; what matters is that He does.

When I thought further about each of the men at the site, each working to do the best they could at their specific job, I had a new appreciation for how God uses us in His master plan. When this new building is complete, it will be a new wing of the hospital: there will be hundreds of new patient rooms, dozens of surgical suites, and hopefully a place of hope and healing for people in our community for years to come. And it's all because this team of dedicated professionals followed the path and the plans set before them while allowing someone else to oversee the grander picture.

God has a master plan for our life, too, and when we do our part in obedience, amazing things can happen. This is how the kingdom of heaven is built while we're still here on earth. When we know our assignment here, we can feel confident that we're part of something bigger, something we can't see or imagine, but something that is part of God's plan. We each have a role to play to further the gospel and to grow Christ's kingdom—

When we know our assignment here, we can feel confident that we're part of something bigger, something we can't see or imagine, but something that is part of God's plan.

that's part of our calling as believers.

So many times, especially as women, we can't understand where we fit in or what our role exactly is, but know this— *you were created for a specific purpose*, a specific role on earth and in the lives of people you touch. No one else on the planet can fulfill this role as you were intended to—it is your destiny to build Christ's Kingdom as He has equipped you.

I've learned four important principles about God's love for us and how it manifests itself. They are:

1. God sees you. In Genesis 16:13, Hagar said this:

"You are the God who sees me... I have now seen the One who sees me.'"

Hagar cried out to God when she had run away from Abraham's house, but God saw her in the desert and rescued her from death. Just like Hagar, God sees you in the deserts of your life and will rescue you, too.

2. God hears you. We know that God hears the cries of our heart, our petitions, and our prayers and He promises to answer whenever we call upon Him. This is the promise of Psalm 91:15:

"'He will call on me, and I will answer him; I will be with him in trouble, I will deliver and honor him.'"

3. God covers you with grace. This means you are granted undeserved favor, no matter your past or what you have ever done wrong. All He asks is our humble repentance as it says in James 4:6:

"...But he gives us more grace. That is why Scripture says: 'God opposes the proud but shows favor to the humble.'"

4. God surrounds you with favor. Two verses from Psalms speak of this holy favor. The first is Psalm 5:12:

"Surely, Lord, you bless the righteous; you surround them with your favor as a shield."

And the other is Psalm 3:3:

"But you, Lord, are a shield around me, my glory, the One who lifts my head high."

God wants to lift your head *high* no matter what has happened in your past. He wants to wipe away any shame or rejection you carry with you, regardless of what you've done or what has been done to you. Too many women feel alone and lonely, sad, ugly, and depressed because of where their life has taken them, but God wants to lift you up to a royal palace of influence.

One of my favorite stories in the Bible is the story of Rahab because it tells the story of God's grace and restoration so beautifully. It comforts me, as it should you, to know that the same love and grace and guidance He provided for Rahab is still available for all of us. It is literally 'ours for the taking.'

Why would we ever refuse such grace and peace and mercy and love?

Read through Rahab's story and see if you can't identify with some of her feelings of unworthiness and guilt and brokenness. And then, see how she is so wonderfully restored.

Rahab was a harlot with a very colorful past who God called to became a woman of dignity. She lived somewhere around the time of 1400 BC, at a time when the Israelites were getting ready to enter the Promised Land. Joshua was now their leader, following in Moses' footsteps.

Joshua sent two spies to Jericho to scope out the land they were pursuing. At the time, Jericho was a bustling, fortified city in the fertile Jordan Valley. It would be no small feat to overtake such a large and established city. When the spies saw the massive fortifications surrounding the city, they knew they would need nothing less than a miracle to capture the city.

The spies entered the city to better understand the layout of the area and to further study the strength of the walls surrounding the city. While in the city, they met and visited with Rahab, the harlot. It is no doubt they were taken by her considerable beauty as she was known as one of the four most beautiful women mentioned in Scripture. (The others are Sari, Abigail, and Esther.) Rahab was a shining example of looks belying a person's heart and happiness. Her striking beauty, when put alongside her dishonorable profession, shows clearly that you can be beautiful on the outside, but completely lost on the inside.

When Rahab first visited with the spies, she told them how all of her city was afraid of the Israelites, "I know that the Lord has given you this land and that a great fear of you has fallen on us, so that all who live in this country are melting in fear because of you" (Joshua 2:9). With that, she asked them to promise to be kind to her family and to spare their lives.

And then *she* protected *them* from danger.

She took them up to the roof of her house and covered them with flax and wheat plants that had been drying in the sun. When the king learned that the spies had been seen going into Rahab's house, he sent his men there to capture them. Rahab explained that she didn't know who they were or that they were spies, but that they had since come and gone, but were probably still close enough to be captured.

After the King's men had left, Rahab instructed the spies to leave by her window (which was part of the city's wall of fortification) and to stay hidden until the soldiers had moved on. Again, she asked for their promise to protect her family: "'Now then, please swear to me by the Lord that you will show kindness to my family, because I have shown kindness to you…'" (Joshua 2:12).

The spies gave her their word and instructed her to make sure all her family was there with her when the attack began and to tie a scarlet rope from the window so the other attackers would know not to harm them. Both Rahab and the spies were true to their respective words as the city was demolished within a few days, but Rahab's home and family were unharmed. When Joshua and his army spared Rahab and her family, she knew in her heart they were from God and that she wanted to know their God.

She acted courageously and unselfishly to protect the spies even though she didn't understand the commitment to their God. But out of this weakness, she was made strong in her faith and given the discernment to understand that she was part of grander plan.

Just like Rahab must have felt like at the time, we can't begin to understand how our decisions *today* affect destiny—ours and others. Even though Rahab was most concerned with the safety and protection of her family, her obedience to the call upon her heart to protect the spies established her as a timeless example of grace and restoration.

But her story doesn't end simply with her protection from the destruction of Jericho. From harlot to woman of godliness, Rahab is transformed in the remaining years of her life. At 50, she converted to Judaism, fell in love, and married a very influential man named Salmon, from the tribe of Judea. Together they had a son named Boaz,

who had a son named Obed,
who had a son named Jessie,
who had a son named David,

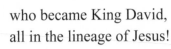

who became King David,
all in the lineage of Jesus!

Think about the complexity and wonder of this—a common harlot from Canaan became a woman of faith, received the privilege of motherhood, and began the lineage of Jesus! Just as He did for Rahab, God has a plan for you—to use you, grow you, and help you to live out your God-given destiny.

God hears each of us. He sees us. He has mercy on us, and he gives us favor. There is a master plan, precious Sleeping Beauty, and you are part of it! Though you may not see it now or understand the process, you are part of a grander, more glorious, plan! Maybe you're the mother or grandmother of the next Billy Graham…or the next President of the United States… or the next great missionary.

There is a master plan, precious Sleeping Beauty, and you are part of it!

Who knows what destiny is waiting for you if you do your part and turn your heart to the one, true God?! You have a future and a hope. Nothing is impossible with our God! Wherever you are now, take hold of the dream and commit to follow Christ. Have the courage to repent and stand for righteousness. God is waiting for you to 'wake up,' beautiful daughter of Zion. When you respond to His call upon your heart, you can be used to help so many other women break free and answer Christ's call upon *their* heart. God *never* rests; He will answer *whenever* you call upon Him.

Finally, remember how I spoke of my intense love for my six grandchildren? They never cease to bring me joy and love and hugs and kisses. And sometimes, a good laugh, too! Not long ago as I was driving with my 10-year-old granddaughter, Alexis, after her dance recital, and my phone rang. Because my phone is hooked up to the Bluetooth service in my car, the caller's name and number appeared on the screen on my dashboard.

It was an incoming call from our Hispanic close friend. He is originally from Puerto Rico and has participated on many mission trips with us. His name is Jesus. Not *the* 'Jesus,' but the Puerto Rican 'Jesus.'

When Alexis saw the name and number, she immediately said, "Oh my goodness, Mimi! You have Jesus' cell phone number?"

A million different answers came to mind, but all I could say was, "Of course, I have His direct line!"

We all have Jesus' direct line. We can call on Him anytime—day or night. We can pour out the fears of our heart, the desires of our life, and everything we hold dear and know that He will hear. And respond.

Your prayers will be heard and answered, Sleeping Beauty, when you awaken to the call of Christ upon your life.

Don't delay and don't resist.

Awaken…and be blessed.

Glenarm Castle

Glenarm, Co. Antrim, Northern Ireland

11

A DREAM COME TRUE

ou've heard the saying, "Once in a while, right in the middle of an ordinary life, love gives us a fairytale"? I'm here to tell you, *it's true*. And it just happened *to me*. Right in the middle of my ordinary, everyday life, I experienced the most magical fairytale *ever.*

It all started about a year ago when we received an invitation to a destination wedding. But this was no usual, beachy, preplanned wedding package sort of event. This was set in Shannon, Ireland. In a castle. For the daughter of a former presidential candidate!

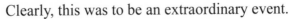

Clearly, this was to be an extraordinary event.

The invitation arrived from our dear friends, Rick and Karen Santorum announcing the upcoming wedding of their daughter, Elizabeth. We've known the Santorums for almost a decade now and had the privilege of watching Elizabeth grow into a beautiful, intelligent, and confident young woman. She met her beloved while studying abroad and so, it seemed natural for them to celebrate in the land that first brought them together.

Everything about the wedding was regal and royal from the start. The wedding was to take place in a 17th-century historic abbey and the celebration afterward in an authentic castle. Our accommodations were to be in a medieval castle called Drumoland near Limerick.

It was the chance of a lifetime—a trip to Ireland, an almost-royal wedding, and nights spent in an honest-to-goodness castle. My heart skipped a beat when I considered going. Needless to say, I was elated when my husband agreed that we shouldn't miss this opportunity.

Once I got the go-ahead that we were going, then the *real* planning got started. I knew I had to have a dress designed and made because an event of this stature most definitely called for something well beyond an off-the-rack, mass-produced dress. I needed original and tailored and one-of-a-kind.

I also got about the business of designing an Irish tweed suit and vest for my husband because he needed something memorable to wear, too! Looking back, I can honestly say that the months of preparation and planning for the days of celebration in Ireland were almost as fun as the events themselves. Almost...but not quite!

The 8+-hour flight from Dallas to Shannon is quite the long haul, but that was all forgotten when we saw the castle where the reception was to take place. In my wildest imagination, I could never have expected it to be so beautiful.

Here's an excerpt from my journal upon our arrival:

"Once in a while, a real, true-life fairytale happens. You're not expecting it, but it finally happens—a little girl's dream of spending the night in a real castle. Tonight, I am in a castle nestled in amongst a shimmering lake and more than 400 acres of lush green grass and tall, ancient trees. The castle is just what you'd expect: towers and long, winding halls laced with red and gold accents. It clearly reminds me of the castle in "Sleeping Beauty" that I've grown up seeing in storybooks.

There are chandeliers sparkling all throughout the grand halls and staircases laced with ornate wooden carvings are hidden in different grand rooms. I literally can't believe that I am in a castle that was home to a family of Irish royalty dating back to the 15th century. (Though, to be totally clear, there were a few additions made to the castle as recently as 1835!). There are 24 bedrooms, numerous elegant dining rooms, parlors, banquet rooms, and even hidden, secret rooms we didn't see.

The castle was in eight generations of the O'Brien family—their ancestral home for almost 200 years. And as I ponder the significance in my heart, I think about my book—this book—and my mandate to 'wake up the sleeping beauties' of the world. I keep thinking of how God loves his daughters so deeply and the

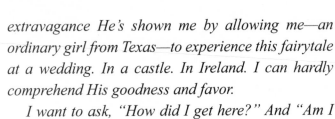

extravagance He's shown me by allowing me—an ordinary girl from Texas—to experience this fairytale at a wedding. In a castle. In Ireland. I can hardly comprehend His goodness and favor.

I want to ask, "How did I get here?" And "Am I dreaming?" The beauty and the joy are almost too much to take in.

The castle is full of shields and shining armors; you can just imagine the stories from the ancient Celtic glory days or the Knights of the Round Table. There are expensive, ornate paintings on every wall and finely woven drapes and carpets throughout to enhance the beauty.

Right now, as I write in my journal, I am looking out my bedroom window, perched high on the third story of the castle. My window is open and a cool breeze is blowing as a light and misty rain begins to fall.

The trees here are strong and green and somewhere between 600 and 700 years old! The grass covering the castle grounds is so emerald green it looks as if it has been painted. In the distance, I see a horse-drawn carriage with two of the most stately, royal horses I have ever seen. There is the smell of fresh flowers filling the room and I can just barely hear Celtic music playing ever-so-softly in the background.

Last night, there was a soft moon glow for most of the night because this is the time of the year when the days are longer. Because of this, it never gets completely dark while we're here; there's even a soft twilight glow at midnight.

I feel an overwhelming sense of peace here in this castle. My roots from my father's side are in this historic land. Higgins was my maiden name and, everywhere I look, there is someone named Higgins. The governor is named Michael Higgins and there's even a store inside the castle named 'Billy Higgins.'

Like most everyone else I know, I am a mixture of several nationalities but for tonight...tonight I am enjoying pretending I am a royal princess. My husband's surname is Pogue and it seems everyone we've met knows that name, too. There's an Irish rock band named Pogue and, in the ancient Irish Celtic language of Gaeilge, Pogue means 'kiss.' It seems so strange to feel like you belong to a place you've never been—especially when everyone you meet seems to recognize your name.

As I gaze out my window again, I can't help but think about the story of 'Sleeping Beauty' and I am reminded that the prince found her after she had been asleep after 100 years. And then—then he woke her with a kiss! It reminds me how there are seasons in our life—times of beautiful sunshine, times of storms, times of gentle winds, and times of rain. Each season of our life brings new surprises and for me, this season is extra special because—here I am—spending the week in an Irish castle!

Tomorrow we go to the wedding in the 17th-century abbey. God is giving me a surprise I didn't expect: In my heart I have a passion to tell women everywhere that God wants them to have a 'wake up' experience. Maybe we can't all have the experience of sleeping in

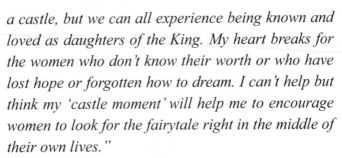

a castle, but we can all experience being known and loved as daughters of the King. My heart breaks for the women who don't know their worth or who have lost hope or forgotten how to dream. I can't help but think my 'castle moment' will help me to encourage women to look for the fairytale right in the middle of their own lives."

So that was my journal entry when I poured out my heart and soul on that rainy day in that beautiful, ancient castle. So many thoughts and prayers and hopes and dreams that were brought to mind in that magical setting.

The next day, we all gathered at the lovely abbey to witness the ceremony. My mind was trying to picture what grand ceremonies had transpired in the 11th century when it was built. During the Medieval Period, many of the people who worked on these abbeys never saw the final church. Most of these structures took over 100 years to build. But today I was able to experience the final architectural plan full of history and romance. The abbey itself was beyond gorgeous. The arched ceilings, incredible stained-glass windows, and massive pipe organ set the stage for a sacred celebration. When Elizabeth walked down the aisle, the bells were ringing, the choir was singing, and the organ filled the abbey with the sweetest sounds of celebration. Elizabeth was completely and utterly a vision and her husband looked every bit the part as her knight in shining armor. His attendants in royal green kilts completed the royal setting.

Later in the evening, the guests gathered again at the castle for the royal ball to celebrate the newlyweds. With more than 200 guests dressed to the nines in ball gowns and tuxedos, it was a scene right out of a movie. So much so, the bride and groom dance to the music from 'Pride and Prejudice.' Every detail throughout the evening reminded me of one romantic movie after another.

There were so many magical moments that night, but probably the most special to me was when the father danced with his daughter, the bride. You could see the love and admiration he held for his daughter. And in my heart, I thought this is how God, Our Heavenly Father, must look at us as *His* daughters and *His* royal brides. Even though we know our faults and shortcomings, all He sees when He looks at us is love and forgiveness and purity.

How joyful life would be if we could accept and embrace His perspective of us and not the world's.

In closing, I want to leave you with another granddaughter story because, truth be told, it's where I get the best and funniest stories.

My daughter-in-law, Jennifer, had just put her newborn daughter, Reagan, down for a nap. On her way from the nursery, she stopped by daughter Alexis' room just to make sure she was resting, too. Sure enough, Alexis was resting quietly on her bed.

Mission accomplished! Two children, a baby and a newly two-year-old, resting at the same time! Hallelujah! With the girls only 16 months apart, life was hectic at their house all day, every day. Jennifer decided to take full advantage of this sweet gift of solitude and went to read in another room. Little did she know, this was Alexis' cue to ditch the nap and scout for treats.

She headed for the pantry and spotted the biggest, most colorful jar of jelly beans ever—on the top shelf. Not to be discouraged, Alexis scaled the shelves, snagged the

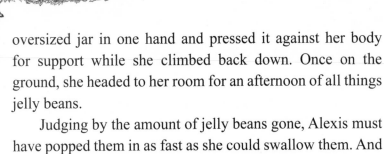

oversized jar in one hand and pressed it against her body for support while she climbed back down. Once on the ground, she headed to her room for an afternoon of all things jelly beans.

Judging by the amount of jelly beans gone, Alexis must have popped them in as fast as she could swallow them. And when she grew tired of eating them, she began to play with them. She smashed them into her carpet, on the walls, and onto her sheets. There were colorful spots *everywhere.*

For whatever reason, Jennifer went and checked on her girls just to be sure they were still napping soundly. And then...then she peeked into Alexis' room. Alexis was covered in jelly beans. Head to toe. Stuck to her face, stuck to her clothes, stuck in her hair. And the ones that didn't stay stuck on her left colorful splotches of pink and blue and red and green and orange on her, the walls, and the carpet.

Without missing a beat, Jennifer stepped into 'mom mode'-- scooped up Alexis, ran some warm bath water, and began washing the sugar stains from her little one's face and hair and body. Within minutes, Alexis was good as new and Jennifer began to tackle the rest of the mess. It was quite the process, eventually involving professional carpet cleaning and a fresh coat of paint, but in the end, it was a marvelous illustration, too—of how Christ washes each of us clean from sin and filth.

I love that story and it's one I'll never forget. It's also a story I've used countless times to drive home the power of Christ in our lives. Most recently, I was speaking at a women's conference in Lima, Peru, and I took the stage with a gallon jar filled with bright colored jelly beans. It was fun to watch the ladies' expressions as they wondered what I was going to do with the jelly beans and how they went together with Jesus.

When I explained the story of Alexis, every mother there could relate to cleaning up messes made by their children. That opened the door to share how Jesus cleans up the messes we make and restores us to better than new afterwards. The altars were full that afternoon as woman after woman came to understand the restorative love and grace of Christ *in their lives.*

In one simple illustration, hundreds of women came to understand that, if a weary mother could so lovingly wash away the mess of her young daughter, how much more does God care for and love us— *His children?*

Sleeping Beauty, know this—we all make mistakes, day after day, moment after moment. At times throughout our lives, we've all felt as if our lives were just one big mess—a mess so big it was beyond repair. But that's simply not true. No one's life is out of reach of God. *Every single time* we turn to Christ for help, He shows us mercy. *Every single time* He washes us clean and forgives us. No

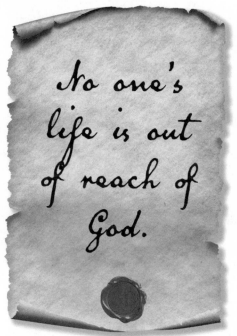

matter what; no matter how many times. When Christ steps in, we become pure and clean *and forgiven.* This is the holy promise of Isaiah 1:18:

"'Come now, let us settle the matter,' says the Lord. 'Though your sins are like scarlet, they shall be as white as snow; though they are red as crimson, they shall be like wool.'"

Isaiah 1:18

I know—I can sense it—that somewhere in this world, you are 'waking up' to the call upon your life. You've been a Sleeping Beauty for far too long. If you are willing to accept it, the Heavenly Father wants to show you *His* glory in *your* life. He wants to take you on a great adventure and make your dreams come true.

You are a royal daughter because you are the daughter of a King. Stand on His word and speak His promises over your life and you will be transformed.

This is <u>your</u> day,
<u>your</u> time,
<u>your</u> life.
<u>You</u> can have an abundant life and experience fairytales that turn into reality.

Powerscourt Estate

Enniskerry, Co. Wicklow, Ireland

12

WOMEN OF INFLUENCE

t may sound crazy, but a movie star captured my outlook on life. Audrey Hepburn was known for her eternally optimistic perspective, her cheerful demeanor, and a glass-half-full way of seeing things. It's a great way to live and how I view each day I'm blessed to be alive.

This is what she said:

"I believe in pink. I believe that laughing is the best calorie burner.

I believe in kissing, kissing a lot.

I believe in being strong when everything seems to be going wrong.

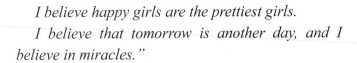

I believe happy girls are the prettiest girls.
I believe that tomorrow is another day, and I
believe in miracles."

Isn't that just the most wonderful way to look at life?

In all my many travels, I have been beyond blessed to meet so many kinds of women *from every walk of life imaginable.* I've met women who live well below the poverty line and women who run companies as presidents and CEOs. I've met women who are mothers, grandmothers, and great-grandmothers and women who have never birthed a baby. And I've met women that have achieved the highest level of education available and some who can hardly read.

And the one common thread between them all? They are *all* powerful. And they were all created to bring love and beauty to those around them.

Even though on many fronts, men and women have similar gifts, more often than not, it is the woman who brings the beauty to a home, an event, or even just a regular day at the office or with the kids. Women and beauty have been inextricably linked from the beginning.

Just for a moment, consider a world without a woman's touch for beauty—both for herself and her surroundings. Most men operate with functionality and efficiency as their top priorities; women want to know how something's going to look or make you feel; we're all about enhancing a relationship, an experience, or a home. Men are much more inclined to build a structure that promotes productivity and helps to make things happen. The truth is our homes would look more like grey army barracks than a castle if men designed them. Women, on the other hand, want to know how something is going to look and how it will it promote togetherness and encourage relationships. It is just the way God miraculously designed women—beauty is a priority with us.

One of my closest friends is an interior designer. She started by decorating small spaces and worked hard to please her clients. When she woke up to the Lord's call upon her life, there was no stopping her. She realized her power was in creating beautiful spaces. Even though it took her years to cultivate and grow a business, she didn't give up. She's since moved to Los Angeles and decorates penthouses and grand estates across the country and the world. And she is in high demand as a designer because she has been faithful and passionate to use her God-given talents to serve her customers.

Not long ago I asked her, "Why do you love what you do so much?"

She replied, "I love to make the world beautiful."

It's that simple. And powerful. Women are called to bring beauty and color and warmth wherever they go.

Women also love to take something old and make it new again. We love to breathe new life into worn and weary things because we see the possibility of their beauty hidden beneath a few layers of old paint or some worn out material or some outdated style. We can't help it—we want to restore beauty where beauty once was, but has faded. It brings us joy whether we are stripping the varnish off an old table or

breathing life and encouragement into the heart of another discouraged woman.

I remember when we first got married, my new husband's little apartment was spotless. It was clean, orderly, and *boring!* The only furniture consisted of a couch, a chair, and a lamp. And his vanity? There was nothing more on his clean, clean vanity than a toothbrush and a bottle of cologne. Needless to say, this sparse existence didn't last too long once I arrived. My husband will be the first to tell you that the day I moved in, *everything changed.* What was once just his space was now *our* space and I intended to make it feel like home—*for both of us.*

By the time I got finished unpacking and displaying all of my lotions, creams, and perfumes, my husband said it looked like I had moved a small city into his very perfect space. And that was *before* I even unloaded my nail polishes, beauty masks, specialty shampoos and conditioners, and more. When I was done, all my products had taken up my share of vanity space and most of his, too! But, in my defense, it did smell like a lovely Polynesian island!

This was just one of the ways I began to wake up my husband. Each of us has our own special way (or ways) we show our love and affection for the men in our lives, but few things can touch the heart of a man like a woman who truly believes in him. Countless songs have been written about the romantic love between a man and a woman; plays and dramas about love are produced each year for Broadway, the movies, and television. There's no shortage of romance novels written each year as well.

But there's one particular way that a woman most effectively speaks to a man's heart and it is through her voice.

I recently met a famous woman attorney who has a network television show which also has extremely high ratings among male viewers. After we had talked for a while I encouraged her to always remember the power in her voice. She looked at me surprised and asked, "Do you really think I have a special power in my voice?"

"Yes! Absolutely," I assured her.

And then I began telling her how men listen to the voices of the women in their lives differently than they listen to men. Just think about how most men respond to their mothers, wives, sisters, and daughters—they usually pay attention to the voices of these important women in their lives. I have experienced the same thing as my television friend. I have noticed that whenever I speak at business conferences, the men consistently listen well and I think it is out of respect for a woman's voice. Men listen differently *to your voice.*

Sleeping Beauties, it is imperative that you realize the influence and power you have been entrusted with.

Sleeping Beauties, it is imperative that you realize the influence and power you have been entrusted with. Since the beginning of time, women have played a major role in shaping society in every way from raising families to discovering inventions to promoting life-saving causes. Women have altered the course of history, worked to save entire countries, and been responsible for carrying the

Gospel of Christ throughout the world. When you consider the accomplishments of women such as Aimee Semple McPherson, Joan of Arc, Amelia Earhart, Queen Victoria, Elizabeth I, Harriet Beecher Stowe, Florence Nightingale, Anne Frank, Helen Keller, and Mother Teresa, their impact and influence spans decades and continents. Even Moses' mother, Jochebed, saved the nation of Israel because she had the courage to put her newborn son in a basket and place him in the Nile River to be found by Pharaoh's daughter. These women are just a few examples of women who have used their passion and talents to shape society and cultures and beliefs since Eve was first created.

And the list of other, *equally accomplished,* women could go on endlessly.

It is also important for women to realize their influence can be used for good or evil. They have the power to cause or lead men to do good and to bring about prosperity and peace for a family, a company, or even a country. Women also have the power to persuade men to commit crimes, become dishonest, or act ill-intentioned towards everyone they meet. It is a serious responsibility to use the power of our love and respect honorably.

Probably one of the more classic cases of the power of love involves Wallis Warfield Simpson and Prince Edward VII. The Prince's love for the twice-divorced Mrs. Simpson was so complete, he gave up his promise to rule as King of England for her. Government officials successfully argued that a divorced woman with two living husbands was politically and socially unacceptable for a woman who could someday be queen. Mrs. Simpson's colorful background was simply too much for the royal family to accept.

Ultimately Prince Edward came to realize that he would have to choose between serving his country as king one day or marrying the woman he loved. He chose her and thus ended his significant place in history. That's the value a man can place on his love for a woman—deep, consuming, and sacrificial love. And, as much of a sacrifice Edward made for Wallis Simpson, consider what Adam gave up in the Garden of Eden—*eternal, sinless life.* It's hard to believe looking back, but that's exactly what happened when Eve offered him a bite of an apple. She made false and misleading promises and convinced an otherwise honorable man to disobey God. Even though Adam knew the apple was forbidden, he chose the words and promises of a deceptive woman over the words and promises of God.

You have a powerful role to play in society.

Hear me, Sleeping Beauties—when you wake up, wake up for good, *not evil!* Whatever your roles in life—wife, mother, business woman, entrepreneur, volunteer—you have a powerful role to play in society. And I promise you this: if you will listen to your heavenly Father and walk in His covenant promises, you will change the course of generations *for good.* You can be both strong and tender; soft, beautiful, gentle, and kind. Believe me when I tell you that men are drawn to women who respect them.

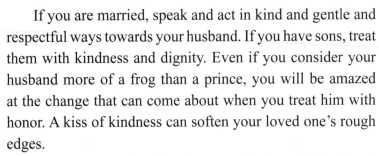

If you are married, speak and act in kind and gentle and respectful ways towards your husband. If you have sons, treat them with kindness and dignity. Even if you consider your husband more of a frog than a prince, you will be amazed at the change that can come about when you treat him with honor. A kiss of kindness can soften your loved one's rough edges.

When my husband and I travelled to Ireland and Scotland recently, I came to learn the history of the Vikings and the role that powerful, yet gentle, women played in transforming these beastly men into civilized gentlemen. It was fascinating to see the impact of a gentle hearts upon so many savage souls.

All the way back to the 8th-century and well into the 11th, the Viking men would sail from Scandinavia to Scotland and Ireland. These men were warriors through and through. Civilized behavior and good manners was not part of their make-up. However, as the years passed and they continued these trips westward, the Viking men began to see and understand a more peaceful and civilized way to live. They saw how many of the Protestant Christians did business— ethically and with honesty—and began to be influenced by it. They even began to learn the Gaelic language and culture.

The result? Many, many of these men turned their hearts towards God and accepted His salvation when they realized that's what was different about the Scottish and Irish people they were meeting. But here is the surprising detail: many of the men who became Christ-followers did so because of the Christian women who had influenced them. The women were treating these unruly men with respect and kindness and the warriors took note. It wasn't long before Christianity began to spread throughout the ranks of these rugged men.

Soon, the Viking men were actively engaged in building the communities where they traded. They helped build churches and townships. And because of their brilliantly engineered ships, they were regarded as highly skilled craftsmen and builders. Their help was invaluable.

Isn't the contrast between these two *completely opposite* kinds of people—men and women, gruff and crude versus kind and refined, aggressive and abrasive up against welcoming and kind—truly remarkable? The Vikings were among the absolute fiercest warriors in European history and yet, when they met godly Celtic women, their hearts were changed to the point of giving up their pagan gods for the one, true God. Soon they began to marry, settle down, and have children.

One at a time, the Sleeping Beauties of the time lived out their faith when dealing with the roughest of the rough. They modeled the love of Christ and, in doing so, armies of men came to kneel before what they came to understand as a loving Savior. This is what love does: it causes the wicked sinner to kneel before the power of a loving Savior named Jesus Christ. The sleeping warrior Vikings woke up to a better, more promising, and eternal life because their souls were touched by godly women.

My dear, dear Sleeping Beauties, I beg you to sleep no more. Wake up and wake everyone else around you up, too. You can change the world around you by opening your eyes to the beauty God has put inside of you. The beauty is there, I promise. It is waiting to be shared.

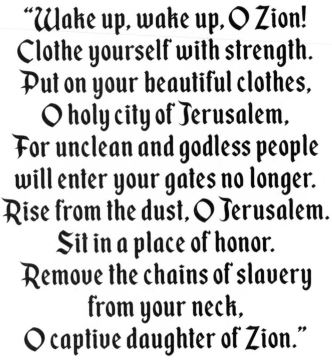

"Wake up, wake up, O Zion!
Clothe yourself with strength.
Put on your beautiful clothes,
O holy city of Jerusalem,
For unclean and godless people
will enter your gates no longer.
Rise from the dust, O Jerusalem.
Sit in a place of honor.
Remove the chains of slavery
from your neck,
O captive daughter of Zion."

Isaiah 52:1-2

To find out more about Judy Pogue and
Pogue Family Mission Society please visit:

JudyPogue.com